MASTERING

upwork

MASTERING
upwork

THE ULTIMATE GUIDE TO ATTRACTING, CONVERTING, AND KEEPING EXCELLENT CLIENTS ON **UPWORK**

BY MIKE VOLKIN

DEDICATION

I dedicate this book to my wife Audrey and offer her my sincerest thanks, for not only allowing, but for also encouraging my entrepreneurial dreams.

I also dedicate this book to the staff at Upwork, who encouraged me to write this and provided fantastic insight.

Lastly, this book would not have been possible without the professional work of Harry Carver, the best copywriter/editor/proofreader/ghostwriter a guy could ask for. You were patient, thorough, careful and a joy to work with. For anyone who might need Harry's services, you can find his Upwork profile here: Upwork.com/freelancers/~018217147a72860031

ISBN: 978-0-578-81148-2

TABLE OF CONTENTS

SECTION 1

INTRODUCTION

WHO AM I?

My name is Mike Volkin, and this is my least favorite section of the book. This is where I have to talk about myself, which I don't like doing because I am a humble person. However, I need to do this so you will understand why you should listen to me.

I am a marketing strategist and entrepreneur coach. And, at the time of this writing, an expert-vetted (top 1%) Upwork freelancer, featured on Upwork's home page.

Like many of you, I was once a newcomer to the freelancing game. Because of my background as a scientist, I approached Upwork freelancing with a different mindset than most—I experimented with everything!

As a scientist, I am trained on how to do tests. So, I analyzed and tested every aspect—every variable involved with being a freelancer. This included countless tests on Upwork's platform. After many iterations of my profile, my photo, titles, hourly rates, proposals, availability, skills, videos, and much more, I learned what worked, what worked better, and what didn't work at all.

I didn't start out as a successful freelancer. I earned dual bachelor's and a master's of science degree. While in college, I spent countless hours in a water chemistry lab performing tests, writing reports and analyzing results. When I graduated, I landed a job and realized I didn't enjoy working for the company. So, I bounced from job to job, convinced it was the company I didn't like, but eventually I realized it was working for someone else that I didn't like. Even then, though, I didn't jump into freelancing full time.

Three days after the tragic events of September 11, 2001, I joined the Army, with zero knowledge of what I was getting myself into. I just felt an urgent need to serve my country. It was an unstoppable urge. My legs practically walked themselves to the recruiter's office. After handing my application to the recruiter, he looked at me, laughed and said, "Why do you want to enlist in the Army? You have a master's degree. Why don't you go the officer route?" I was so naïve I didn't even know what that meant. In civilian words, he meant, "you're about to take the hard road, son." A few weeks later I was eyeball to eyeball with a drill sergeant in basic training, seriously doubting the choices I made. But I dug in, adapted, and gave 100% of everything I had. Six months later, I was an honors graduate with a specialty in Nuclear, Biological and Chemical Warfare training. Not long after that, I was in Iraq, where I spent a year fighting in Operation Enduring and Iraqi freedom. I returned with an Army Commendation Medal (probably my most coveted achievement to date). What impact did this have on my freelancing? It gave me the confidence and leadership skills I needed to take command of my career. Ever since then, I have been an entrepreneur and freelancer.

Before becoming a full-time freelancer, I built and sold 4 companies and authored several books (one bestseller). Some might consider that a success, but I didn't. Some might say that makes me smarter than the average person, but I'm not. I never achieved above average grades in school. In high school, I graduated in the 50th percentile of my class, and I scored in the bottom 20% on my SATs. During my first two years in college, I was on academic probation with a GPA of less than 2.0, and I studied my ass off. Success has little to do with intelligence. Success is all about focus, setting goals, tenacity and perseverance—all of which are achievable by anyone.

Know what you want, set ambitious goals and go after it with all that you have, otherwise you will never achieve your highest expectations.

Live by that phrase and you will live a very fulfilled life.

You will learn that buying this book is the best decision you can make for your freelancing career—doubling, tripling, even quadrupling your earnings or more! All you have to do is apply what you learn here.

Some additional points—although Upwork centric, what you will learn in this book applies to other freelance platforms.

Freelancing is a romantic concept. It invokes visions of financial independence, freedom to work from exotic places, and the joy of entrepreneurship—being your own boss! Sounds wonderful, but there are also harsh realities with which all freelancers must contend.

Being a freelancer also means that you are in business for yourself, bearing full responsibility for your success—or failure.

Providing you with the knowledge you need in order to avoid failure is precisely why I wrote this book. As we know, knowledge is power, and, with the information in the following pages, you will achieve the ability to command and control almost every aspect of your freelancing career, from attracting clients, to converting clients, and, most importantly, to keeping clients.

So, what are you waiting for? Start reading—start earning!

UPDATED CONTENT

Upwork is a dynamic enterprise, constantly improving, growing, and striving to meet the changing needs of freelancers and employers alike.

Changes, large and small, may occur or have occurred since I published this book.

As a service to my readers, I maintain the following website to keep you informed of said changes: https://freelancermasterclass.com/upworkmasterybook.

WHY FREELANCE?

Freelancing is an attractive income option for many reasons, however, the three principal factors in choosing a freelancing career are 1) the ability to control your own schedule, 2) no upper limit on earnings, and 3) being able to take advantage of a broad variety of opportunities.

Other advantages include the ability to work from home, the beach, or your favorite coffee shop. If you live in a developing country, freelance work can give you access to higher pay than you might find in local job markets.

It is also a plus to put that punishing commute to work behind you. In the U.S., the average, one-way commute time is 26.1 minutes, according to the U.S. Census Bureau. So a commute to and from work averages 52 minutes. If you have no commute, that's a lot of time savings. Do you know what I can do in 52 minutes? Here are some examples:

- Workout/stretch/yoga,
- Educate myself on my craft,
- Prospect for more work,
- Watch my favorite TV show,
- Spend more time with my family,
- Get a billable hour in (almost),
- Mediate/creative visualization,
- Sleep in,
- and so much more.

Given that there are 20 workdays in a month, that's 17 hours a month of extra free time. Don't let it go to waste.

If you live in a developing country, freelance work can give you access to higher pay than you might find in local job markets. I know many freelancers in countries that would typically earn $10-$20/hour working for local clients but can charge $50/hour, or more, for clients in the U.S. because they specialize in a skill that U.S. companies find highly desirable. Such freelancers use platforms like Upwork to find great job opportunities.

In short, there are as many reasons to choose a career in freelance work as there are individuals.

EQUIPMENT YOU NEED

No *one-size-fits-all* equipment list exists, because the variety of services freelancers offer is extensive. However, everyone will need:

- a reliable Internet service provider;

If you have qualms about the quality of your service, take an Internet speed test. This service is available free, through multiple providers, easily found with a Google search.

- a laptop/desktop computer with adequate storage and RAM for your work;
- software, specific to the services you offer;
- a printer, preferably a combo model, with scanning, copying, and printing functions;
- a desk, sufficiently sized to meet your needs;
- a comfortable office chair—ergonomic, and supportive of good body posture; and
- miscellaneous small office supplies—stapler, paper clips, paper, pens, pencils, etc.

SET GOALS

I cannot stress strongly enough the importance of setting goals for your freelance business. Honestly, how can you measure your progress unless you establish goals? You must *inspect* what you *expect*!

I've made this easy for you by including a spreadsheet to track your progress. You will find access to it here: https://freelancermasterclass.com/upworkmasterybook.

You will need to answer the following questions to complete your Goal Setting spreadsheet:

1.] What is your annual income target?

2.] What percentage of this income is from Upwork, from another freelance platform, and/or from your full or part-time job? (The percentages must total 100 percent)

3.] What is your hourly rate?

When you enter your *total yearly revenue goal*, the spreadsheet calculates your monthly *revenue goal* automatically. Once you enter the remaining values, the spreadsheet calculates the hours you need to work per month, per week, and per day (based upon a 5-day work week) to meet your goal. At this point, you can begin fine-tuning the spreadsheet to ensure that your goals are realistic.

I recommend a maximum 6-hour workday. This allows you up to two hours each day to prospect for work. Regular prospecting, searching and applying for jobs, is not only key to meeting your goals but also improves your ranking in client searches.

Your hours per month should be about 120, but no more than 160. Remember, any hours above 120 cuts into your job prospecting time and it is crucial that you are always prospecting, no matter how busy you are. Some of my best opportunities have come when I am at my busiest. When you're busy and you have more work you can accept, this is your chance to raise your rates. It's the concept of supply and demand. When you are in high demand, you raise your rates!

Turning your attention to the *Billable Hours Log* portion of the spreadsheet, it is important to note that you are recording actual billable hours. This section of the spreadsheet is not intended to reflect currency—hours only! Since the Upwork work week ends at midnight on Sunday, to ensure consistency, it would be best to record your billable hours for the week after midnight on Sunday and before you begin any work for the coming week.

The onboarding list, which occupies the right-hand side of your spreadsheet, is where you will enter your client's name, and the estimated hours per month devoted to that client. The rate comes from the amount you previously entered into the *Hourly Rate* cell.

I'm going to contradict myself and tell you that occasionally you may need to change the hourly rate in the onboarding list to reflect the terms of your agreement with the client. As a practical matter, not all clients will pay the same rate. With fixed-rate clients, you will need to calculate the number of hours manually. Do this by dividing the fixed-rate by your hourly rate. For example, if you have a fixed-rate client that is paying $50.00 for the job and your hourly rate is $25.00, the number of hours you will enter is 2 (50/25=2).

The onboarding list serves to track clients and give you a fair estimate of your potential monthly earnings and total hours worked per month. This information appears in the upper right-hand portion of the spreadsheet. These cells are color-coded. Red shows that you are short of your goal, and green shows you are at or above your goal.

Believe me when I tell you using this spreadsheet is the single best thing you can do for your business. If nothing else, tracking your activity with this spreadsheet will reduce your stress and relieve your anxiety, even if you don't meet your goals, but you will, because you are reading this book.

Revenue goals are important, and while that is typically going to be your first consideration, don't lose sight of other goals crucial to your success. For example, life goals, key performance indicators, your schedule, and continuing education (learning). If you aren't learning, you're falling behind!

It's also important to reward yourself for your successes. A nice dinner out, a weekend getaway, or a lazy afternoon at the beach, for example. You work for yourself, so if you don't reward your accomplishments, who will?

WHY FREELANCING IS THE BEST JOB IN THE WORLD

When you have the best job in the world, you can wear what you like, work the hours you want to work, make the income you deserve, be your own boss, leave office politics in the rear-view mirror, and work from anywhere you like, and fulfill your life's purpose. That is freedom!

As an in-demand freelancer, you have the luxury to accept only the work you want, and the work that makes you happiest, working with clients you love.

As a freelancer, you can earn much more money as compared to a corporate job because your potential is unrestrained by a boss, a corporation, or corporate culture.

Freelancing presents you with an opportunity for personal and professional growth unmatched in the salaried world, where you are often siloed—limited to using only a few specific skills. Five years of experience as a freelancer is the functional equivalent of 20 years of experience in the salaried world. The result is that you will be more confident in your work and in your life. I've been freelancing for well over a decade, and I've served over 400 clients. I can't name very many marketers who have experience working in over 36 industries with clients in over 20 countries. The experience I have gained is absolutely unmatched in the corporate world.

You will enjoy greater job security as a freelancer, and you will meet and work with a broader range of people than you can imagine.

A freelance career provides you freedom, with enjoyable, fulfilling work, with the opportunity for a better income, with unlimited personal and professional growth, and with greater job security than those in a private sector, salaried position can ever hope to have.

Wait! Did you say GREATER job security?

Yes! Many people just default to being a corporate employee because that is what their parents did, that is what their friends did, and that is what most of society does, because it's comfortable and secure.

If you are a skilled freelancer, you have more security than you would at a corporate job.

If you get fired from your one corporate job, what percentage of employed are you? The answer is zero. If you are a freelancer with 10 clients, and you lose one client, what percentage of employed are you? The answer is 90%. You still have income and you can get another client.

The worst part about being a corporate employee is the risk of getting fired for things completely outside of your control. Just look at what happened in 2020 with the COVID-19 pandemic. Millions of people lost their jobs. Conversely, many freelancers thrived.

For these compelling and factual reasons, in my opinion, freelancing is the best job in the world.

YES... FREELANCING CAN SUCK SOMETIMES

Freelancing isn't all rainbows and unicorns. Every occupation has its drawbacks, and freelancing is no exception. Here are some reasons freelancing sucks:

Competition

Recent estimates place the number of freelancers, globally, at around 1.1 billion. That is 35 percent of the world's workforce. Experts predict that number will grow to 80 percent of the global workforce by 2030. In a word, competition is exploding!

Overcoming your competition is best accomplished by branding yourself in a niche that aligns with your passion. If you are good at what you do, have a prospecting system in place, and know how to close and service clients, you won't have to worry too much at all about your competition.

Self-motivation

Freelancers have no taskmaster and, for many, that is part of the attraction to freelance work. However, in the absence of a boss, getting motivated to do the work, is a problem for many others.

I believe those who are motivated to freelance are individuals who know in their gut a regular job is not for them.

Self-motivation may not be part of your DNA. In that case, you will need to read self-help books about motivation and/or take self-motivation courses. You can learn to motivate yourself!

Loneliness

Most freelancers work alone. Many find this to be a tough adjustment, and loneliness is a common complaint. The famous artist, Vincent Van Gogh said, "A great fire burns within me, but no one stops to warm themselves at it, and passers-by only see a wisp of smoke."

I think what Van Gogh meant was that no one listens, which is a common complaint I hear from the freelance community.

There are ways to overcome loneliness. For example, you could follow the path of countless freelancers and work from the local coffee shop, or rent space in a co-op office near you.

Work/life Balance

Achieving a work/life balance is not a problem unique to freelancers. People in all professions struggle, to some extent, with drawing the line between their work lives and their personal lives. However, freelancers are vulnerable because most work from home.

This means freelancers must learn to manage distractions. Although this can be difficult if you have children, pets, or an elderly person in your home, but—lines must be drawn!

Another distraction arises when freelancers achieve some success. Suddenly, everything becomes an opportunity, at which point everything can become a distraction. It is important that you don't allow success to throw you from the path that earned you that success. You should embrace and pursue opportunities, but not by jeopardizing the success that is working for you.

Finding Clients

One of the greatest hurdles and major source of stress facing freelancers is finding clients. When you work for someone else, it's their burden to find clients or customers, not yours. Gaining the skills needed to find clients is an absolute necessity. I will address this in greater detail later in the book.

Adjusting to the Hours

If you enter freelancing from the typical 9-to-5 work environment, you will face adjustments. For example, your client may be on the other side of the globe, in a completely different time zone. Your client's Saturday may not have started, but yours is half over. Or, while you may be ready for bed, your client's workday is just starting.

In my experience, it is best to avoid taking the same days off as other freelancers. Take different days off—don't forego days off. Taking time away from work is important for your mental and physical well-being.

You should have set hours and let your client know your work schedule up front. Make it clear to your prospects when you work and when you don't. If they email you when you're not working, they won't expect a fast response. Lack of communication is the biggest factor souring a client relationship. In many respects, doing a poor job for a client, but communicating well is the same as doing a superb job but not communicating well.

Lack of Corporate Benefits

Speaking of well-being, another downside of freelancing is the lack of benefits, such as paid time off, sick days, health insurance and paid vacation time. This makes it critically important that you diligently manage your health and fitness.

Difficult Conversations

Many of us are hard-wired to avoid confrontation. Freelancing requires that you discuss your pay, your scope of work, and reasonable deadlines with your client. These can be stressful conversations. The good news is that experience will resolve these problems, even to the point where such negotiations are rarely necessary.

THE UPS AND DOWNS
OF FREELANCING

As I said earlier, freelancing is not all rainbows and unicorns. Like most pursuits, freelancing has both positive and negative aspects. Let's get an overview of the upsides and downsides of freelance work.

The Upsides

- Freelancing has minimal start-up costs. In most cases, prospective freelancers already have the equipment they need.

- You can pursue more than a single line of work. For example, you may offer writing services and proofreading, or illustration and design. Freelancing gives you the flexibility to pursue many passions, whereas corporate work is often siloed to a specific skill set.

- Because you set your own hours, you can start freelancing part-time (often referred to as a side-hustle), while maintaining full-time employment. You have the freedom to transition to full-time freelancing whenever you achieve the comfort level to do so.

- Working where you want and when you want, from the comfort of home, a cooperative office space, the corner coffee shop, or the local library. You get to set your own hours, with no time parameters to work within. Your only time sensitive obligations are the client deadlines.

- Imagine telling your boss that you really do not care for that assignment and would prefer to work on something else. Such a statement could earn you a shortcut to the unemployment line in the corporate world. However, freelancers are free to turn down clients, and even the tasks clients assign. Freelancing gives you the, here's that word again, freedom to take a pass on work that you don't enjoy.

- Variety in your work is an upside that receives less attention than it deserves. Variety not only makes your work more interesting, it also helps you learn and grow professionally and personally. If after being a full-time freelancer you decide to return to a corporate job, your work experience will blow away anyone you're up against for a job.

- By avoiding the daily commute, you can save money that you would otherwise spend on fuel, vehicle maintenance, tolls, parking, or train & bus fare. Incidentally, no commute helps the environment and reduces your carbon footprint.

- Speaking of savings, as a freelancer you avoid the expense of maintaining a separate professional wardrobe, and the cost of meals, coffee, and snacks purchased away from home, which can add up to hundreds of dollars over the course of the year. I've had many web meetings with freelancers who are working in their pyjamas, which is a perfectly acceptable dress code when meeting with certain people (not prospects or clients though).

The Downsides

- Even established freelancers experience ebbs and flows in income. When you work a salaried job, you know what your earnings will be at the end of the pay period. Freelancers do not! This can be stressful and result in no small measure of anxiety. This is the reason I developed the Goal Setting spreadsheet—to help you overcome that stress and anxiety. I believe the single biggest reason those with corporate jobs decline to pursue their freelancing passion, is because they fear inconsistent income.

- Freelancers, at least those working in the USA, pay income tax. These taxes will be a higher percentage of your income than you might expect. When you are on someone's payroll, the employer pays around 50 percent of your tax burden as payroll taxes. Being self-employed, you handle 100 percent of your income tax obligation. The IRS requires you to pay quarterly, estimated tax payments, besides filing your 1040 by the April deadline. Don't worry about understanding taxes as a freelancer, getting a good bookkeeper is all you need to do. A good bookkeeper will remind you of what payments are due and when. Later in the book I will show you how to save for taxes so there are no surprises when you write those checks to the state and federal government.

- Most self-employed individuals work more than a forty-hour week. If you turned to full-time freelancing so you could work less, you may have made a mistake. However, if you position yourself correctly, it doesn't feel like work.

- Sadly, not all clients are worthy of your trust. Clients can be problematic, demanding, and may vanish without paying you for completed work, yet another reason I am a proponent of Upwork. They have a payment protection plan for freelancers. Later in the book, I'll teach you prospect vetting techniques and which prospects you should avoid.

- Time management is crucial for freelancers. The freedom you enjoy can lead to procrastination. If you lack self-control and do not develop time-management skills, trouble is on the horizon. Stay motivated by taking regular breaks and allowing time for yourself. Are you a morning person or a night owl? Find the schedule that works for you and procrastination will be less of an issue. I did a Facebook live event on how to avoid distractions. You can view it at: https://freelancermasterclass.com/upworkmasterybook.

YOU ARE A BUSINESS— TREAT YOURSELF LIKE ONE

Like it or not, as a freelancer you are a business, and that carries a unique set of responsibilities from those you had as a salaried worker bee. Sure, you are your own boss, but don't lose sight of the fact that you are also the accountant, the marketing director, the HR department, the worker bee and more!

You *are* a business and you need to act like one before things get out of hand. It is your responsibility to make everything happen and to keep everything running smoothly.

Treating your freelance career like a business is essential to its growth and financial success. Approaching freelancing as a business serves several strategic purposes.

First, a business mindset will encourage you to approach your work professionally. You will be more inclined to meet deadlines and consider your client's needs. You will also recognize the importance of planning and growing your client base.

A business approach means keeping your business and personal finances separate. Consider carving out a paycheck for yourself, rather than co-mingling the proceeds of your freelance work in your personal account. This will be a significant benefit to you come tax time and will also help you mitigate the ebbs and flows in your income stream that I spoke about earlier.

The way you approach your relationship to others is key to your business success, especially on Upwork, where each client can publicly review you. Former UFC champion Frank Shamrock has a strategy for building relationships that he refers to as "Plus, Minus, and Equal."

For the Plus, find someone more successful than yourself, not necessarily monetary success, but your definition of success. Look for someone with the qualities you want to achieve, a person at the level where you want to be at some point. This is an individual that would make a great mentor.

Frank defines a Minus as someone he can teach. Teaching not only helps a Minus, but also helps you increase your understanding of what you're teaching. After all, you can't effectively teach a subject unless you know it inside and out. This is especially important if you are, or want to be, an agency owner. Owning an agency will put you on the phone selling to prospects rather than being in the weeds carrying out projects. Having a Minus to mentor allows you to stay educated on things that may have changed in your industry, or on a specific software program that is important to your clients (or your business).

Frank refers to an Equal as a peer—someone with whom you can share feedback as you scale your business. These shared struggles and success stories build on mutual experiences and inform future decisions for even better outcomes.

The people you choose as a Plus, Minus, and Equal may change frequently because as you reach your goals you will set new ones. For example, if your goal was to have a side-hustle that earns $25,000 one year, your next year's goal could be to be a full-time freelancer earning $100,000. The next goal may be to scale to $250,000. Each of those milestones creates a need for a new Plus, Minus, and Equal.

Start networking now to find a Plus, Minus, and Equal. Beginning this process will put the wheels in motion to treat your business like a business.

UNDERSTANDING CONNECTS AND UPWORK'S FEE STRUCTURE

Connects

Connects are Upwork's cryptocurrency, and you can buy them for a few cents each. Every job you apply for on Upwork displays the number of Connects required to apply for the job—between one and six.

Each Freelancer Basic account receives 10 free *Connects* every month, while the Freelancer Plus plan provides 80 connects per month.

Unused *Connects*, up to 200, will automatically roll over each month. The Freelancer Plus option is best for those new to the platform, because you are unlikely to receive invitations until you have fleshed out your JSS. Invitations to submit proposals require no *Connects*.

Upwork rewards freelancers (and agencies) with 10 free *Connects* each time a proposal is submitted, an interview is won and a response is given. Upwork caps this at a maximum of 50 *Connects* per seven days.

As a new freelancer, when you successfully register with Upwork, you will receive 80 *Connects*, and the opportunity to win an additional 40 *Connects* when you successfully complete the *Upwork Readiness Test*.

Considering the cost of purchasing 80 *Connects*, the few extra dollars you pay each month for the Freelancer Plus plan is easy to justify, given the five additional perks you receive as a Freelancer Plus member:

1.] Prevents Upwork from hiding your profile in the event of extended inactivity.

2.] Allows you to customize your profile URL.

3.] Displays the low, high and average bid on any job.

4.] Permits you to activate a setting that keeps your earnings private, which is a tremendous benefit should you decide to raise your rates (which you will want to do after reading this book). Prospects won't question why you're charging them more because they won't know.

5.] Provides extended reports and enhanced functionality.

When Upwork introduced the concept of *Connects*, freelancers took to the Internet and complained—loudly. Comments streamed through forums and sites like Reddit, claiming Upwork did this to get more money and squeeze every dime from the freelance community. I, on the other hand, couldn't have been happier. Those who complained didn't understand why Upwork implemented *Connects*.

Let's review some pros and cons of paying for *Connects*.

Pros

- Competition for jobs will decrease.
- Clients will find it easier to sort through applications.
- Only freelancers genuinely interested in the job will apply.

Cons

- Freelancers shoulder an expense to apply for work.
- Clients may have fewer applicants for jobs.

As a freelancer, I don't mind paying for *Connects*. Without Upwork, professional freelancers could spend as much as 12 percent of their revenue prospecting for new clients, and this assumes freelancers have the marketing expertise needed to prospect for clients.

Imagine not having platforms like Upwork and having to track down your own prospects. A new freelancer, with little to no network, would have a tough road ahead. Sure, you could set up complicated marketing funnels that start with paid ads on Facebook and Google. You could also try networking and growing an audience on social media. These are arduous processes that take copious amounts of time. These are tactics that require skills. Paying a few cents for each *Connect* is nothing to complain about when you consider your alternatives.

Besides, it weeds out competitors who aren't serious about the job in the first place, and your application gets more attention as a result. It's a no-brainer in my book.

As a client who does a lot of hiring on Upwork, I view *Connects* as a tremendous benefit. Gone are the days when I would post a job for a developer and be slammed with over 50 applicants who didn't even read my job post. The quality of applicants has improved dramatically.

As a freelancer, I'll gladly pony up a few cents to have my proposal taken seriously.

Upwork's Fee Structure

A business only exists if it can turn a profit. Upwork is a business and without sustained profits could not exist. Upwork does not charge freelancers a registration fee, it doesn't clutter its platform with annoying ads, and it doesn't spam your mailbox. What Upwork does is take 20 percent of your earnings. Once you have reached the threshold of $500 in lifetime earnings from a client, Upwork reduces the fee to 10 percent and when you reach $10,000 in lifetime earnings with a client, the rate drops to 5 percent.

As a freelancer, I appreciate that I do not need to spend my time (and money) browsing job boards, placing ads, or maintaining a website. Upwork does that for me, and with greater efficiency than I could reasonably expect to achieve on my own.

How can you put a price on the convenience of simply logging in to Upwork and browsing the hundreds, if not thousands, of jobs that Upwork has already sourced for you? More to the point, you only pay Upwork if you earn. There are no mandatory upfront fees on the platform.

So at first, Upwork's fees may seem pricey. Twenty percent is a big bite out of anyone's paycheck! However, you must look at these fees realistically. You're a businessperson, an entrepreneur, and you need to market your services, right?

Marketing is an expense, and statistics show that businesses spend anywhere from 5 to 12 percent of their gross revenues in marketing costs. Business to business (B2B) firms spend closer to the high-end, and you know what? You are a B2B enterprise!

My point being, it is not unreasonable to view ten percent of the fees you pay to Upwork as a marketing expense that any business would incur in the ordinary conduct of business. But what about the other ten percent, you ask?

Great question! I view this portion of the Upwork fee as an insurance premium. Upwork's hourly and fixed-rate protection programs guarantee payment for your work, providing you follow all applicable rules. Feeling better about those fees? No! Then simply increase your hourly or fixed price by 20% and stop fussing about it!

I was a freelancer long before Upwork came into the scene, and I'll tell you, it was pricey and time-consuming sourcing clients. Sometimes I would put together marketing campaigns that cost thousands of dollars and have no revenue to show for it. That's the mental equivalent of trying to touch the bottom of your foot with the back of your head, it's hard to imagine and it hurts like hell.

SECTION 2

ATTRACT

PICK A NICHE

To ensure we are all on the same page, I will define *niche* in freelancer terms. A niche is similar to a specialty. Medical doctors, for example, specialize in certain aspects of the medical profession. They may specialize in treating cancer (oncology), they may specialize in surgery, they may further specialize in cardiac surgery, to name just a few examples. Lawyers also specialize. They narrow their practice to corporate law, torts, criminal law, family law, wills, personal bankruptcy, and more!

Why do doctors and lawyers find a niche—a specialty? They do so for the identical reasons you should do it. They enjoy the work. They are very good at it. They can develop a level of expertise that earns them a solid reputation, which will allow them to charge higher fees. Freelancers select a niche for the same reasons.

I know what you're saying to yourself, "But if I choose a niche, won't I be alienating all those people who want to hire me?" It would seem that way but the answer is no. There are many millions of dollars to make in just about any niche you can imagine. If you specialize in a niche, everything you do will be centered around attracting the right client. Some of the major advantages to being in a niche are:

- Your messaging will speak perfectly to your prospect.
- You will increase your perceived (and actual) value.
- You will be able to make more money per hour, or per project.
- You will be able to more easily convert prospects into clients.

These are the steps you should follow to define your niche, while making it sufficiently specific to filter out potential clients that are not compatible with the services you offer. Focus on a specific deliverable, and/or a specific industry, always mindful of the sweet spot that is the nexus of your interests, passions, and skills with your target client's needs.

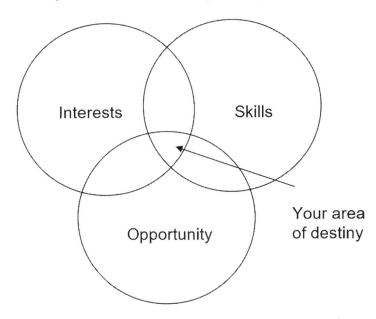

If you haven't already done so, identify your interests, passions, and skills.

An effective niche is one that incorporates your interests, your passions, and your skills. Securing jobs that align with your interests, feed your passions, and comport with your skill set changes the dynamic of work completely. Work is no longer drudgery; it is a joy! When you are happy in your work, you naturally accomplish it more quickly, and with greater precision.

Understand how your interests, passions, and skills can solve a client's problems.

To be effective in your niche, you must appeal to prospective clients. You accomplish this by demonstrating exactly what your unique skill set contributes to solving the prospective client's problem(s). You can explain how you will solve the problem(s) in your proposal, and you must likewise describe it in the text of your profile. I'll have more for you on this in the *Optimizing Your Profile* section later in the book.

Research your competitors.

After you've finished steps one and two, you need to research the competition you will face in the niche you have chosen. Begin by searching freelancer profiles that match your chosen niche. In the ribbon that appears at the top of Upwork pages, you will see a search box. Click on the arrow and select *Browse Talent*, then click the search icon. The freelancers listed represent all categories of talent. Use the *Filter By* options to narrow the field to those freelancers that most closely identify with your proposed niche, and that mirror your skills.

Continue your research as you apply for jobs in your niche. The prospect's job posting contains a wealth of information, especially if the individual or company posting the job has previously hired on the platform. You should pay particular attention to the freelancers the prospective client hired previously. If the freelancer's name appears in green text, all you need to do is click on their name to see their profile. If the freelancer's name is not in green text, that means their profile is private or they are no longer on Upwork. By looking at the profiles of previous hires, you can get a sense of what may have attracted the client to that freelancer, what the freelancer earned on the job, how the freelancer rated the client, whether the client has hired this freelancer in the past, and other valuable information.

I encourage you to undertake this research for at least thirty days, take notes, and look for patterns. Incorporate what you have learned into your profile, your title, possibly even your hourly rate. In short, put what you learned through your observations to work.

Make an assessment of the potential earnings available in your chosen niche.

In the course of your research, you will also get a general idea of what working in your niche pays. This will give you, at the very least, a baseline for the earnings you can expect to receive. This, in combination with the number of jobs, a statistic that appears next to this symbol 🔊 in the top left of the search page, and the number of proposals that jobs in your niche receive, will provide you valuable information regarding the earnings and hiring potential in your chosen niche.

Test your idea.

This is where the rubber meets the road. After having decided upon your interests, passions, and skills, understanding how they are used to meet client needs, researching the competition (and potential clients), and assessing your earnings potential, you must put your findings to the test, tracking the frequency with which your proposals results in hires, how often you receive invitations to interview, and determining whether your earnings are meeting expectations.

Don't worry! Choosing a niche doesn't have to be permanent. Your interests, desires and goals will change over time, and so should your niche.

Go to https://freelancermasterclass.com/upworkmasterybook/ to download a worksheet on how to find your niche.

DETERMINE YOUR HOURLY RATE

Let me say this at the outset, the hourly rate you select for your profile is not nearly as important as the overall quality of your profile. Hourly rates are all over the map in Upwork and if you review as few as 10 random profiles you will be hard-pressed to understand how these freelancers determine their rate.

For example, I just ran a search for Marketing Strategists and found hourly rates ranging from $13 per hour to $240 per hour on the first page of the search results. The average hourly rate for these ten freelancers worked out to around $112 per hour. And before you say anything about their locations, 7 of the 10 are from the United States, and only one is from a developing country, and that freelancer was not the one to offer the lowest hourly rate!

I'm not saying that you should just plug in a number, but of all the concerns you will confront as you pull your profile together, this is not among the top five. After all, as you bid for jobs through the proposal process, you are going to be making an individual assessment as to the value of your work on a case-by-case basis. The hourly rate you post in your profile is a placeholder. However, it is important that the placeholder you settle on is credible. You don't want to drive prospective clients away by charging an exorbitantly high hourly rate or by posting an hourly rate that is so low your reliability and skill set will be in doubt.

Arriving at a decision about what hourly rate to charge begins with some basic research and the exercise I shared with you earlier isn't a terrible place to start. If you price yourself properly, you improve your chances of winning better-paying jobs with great clients.

Your hourly rate not only speaks to your ability; it also reflects your perceived value. Prospective clients usually regard freelancers that charge higher rates as being of higher quality, they attract higher paying work and they earn more.

Another exercise you can try to test your rate involves creating a client account in Upwork. This is easy to do. Just click on settings, scroll down to *Additional Accounts*, click on the *New Client Account* button, and follow the prompts. Then, create a job in your niche and select two freelancers, one with a low rate and one with a high rate. Make sure that both offer the same service in the same niche, have a similar JSS, have worked on Upwork for about the same time, and are both from the United States. In most cases, the freelancer with the higher hourly rate out earns the low rate freelancer. So, what does this tell you?

It suggests that clients view the freelancer with a higher rate as being superior. This is the client's perceived valuation of the freelancer.

Of course, clients can't know which is the better freelancer until they've hired them and the freelancer completes the job. All a client can do is assess the facts and make an educated guess. So creating perceived value is important. If you position yourself to appear more valuable, you increase your chance of being hired, while avoiding those clients who place a premium on price over value. I'll have more on this topic later in the book.

The most important factors in securing work are your proposal letter, your work samples, the quality of your overall profile, and client satisfaction.

Determining your hourly rate on Upwork isn't that tough. It's just a matter of understanding what clients will pay for your service. Upwork provides all the information you need—all you have to do is look for it.

For the sake of illustration, let's assume you are considering freelancing and need to replace your current take-home of $50,000/year. If you are working in the U.S., about 30 percent of your earnings go for taxes, but your employer pays 15 percent of those taxes. This means you will need to earn an additional $15,000 annually to cover your tax liability.

Freelancers may also need to shoulder the costs of their health insurance, business insurance, hardware, software, business supply purchases, and marketing expenses.

Below is a sample of the *Hourly Rate Calculator,* the Excel worksheet I provide for you to download at: https://freelancermasterclass.com/upworkmasterybook/.

How to Calculate Your Hourly Rate	
Current salary or yearly goal	$75,000
Revenue per week	$1,500
Needed to save for payroll taxes/year (15%)	$11,250
Insurance cost/year (Estimated - Can Vary)	$12,000
Business expenses	$4,800
Marketing	
Total	*$103,050*
Work weeks/year	**50**
Hours/week worked	**20**
Revenue needed per week	$2,061
Your hourly rate should be	*$103.05*

It's also a good idea to pad your rate by 10 percent to counter the inevitable *dry spells* that you will experience in your freelancing career. Remember, you have the power to raise or lower the hourly rate in your proposal.

NINETEEN ELEMENTS THAT WILL MAKE YOUR UPWORK PROFILE ROCK

Everyone understands the importance of first impressions, and that is the definition of your profile—a first impression. Until you complete your first job, your profile may contain the only information your prospect can know about you, your services and your abilities. For these reasons, a well thought out profile is crucial to your success.

Fill out every part of your profile. Take full advantage of this opportunity to introduce yourself to prospective clients.

Every Upwork profile includes these elements:

1.] Photo
2.] Name
3.] Location
4.] Job Success Score (JSS)
5.] Badges
6.] Total Earnings / Hours Worked
7.] Number of Jobs (*Completed* and *In Progress*)
8.] Title
9.] Introduction / Bio / Overview

10.] Hourly Rate

11.] Video (Optional)

12.] Availability

13.] Employment History

14.] Other Experiences

15.] Languages

16.] Verifications

17.] Education

18.] Testimonials (Employers outside of Upwork) | Certifications and Awards

19.] Skills (Tags)

We will examine each of these elements, one-by-one, and I will provide you with insights, suggestions, and the resources necessary for you to create your best profile. Obviously, there are elements of your profile over which you will have no direct control, such as your name and your location. However, as you will learn, you have direct or indirect control of most of these elements.

Before you complete your profile, I strongly recommend a thorough review of Upwork's *Terms of Service*. This will save you potential grief down the road. It's important, because violating Upwork's *Terms of Service* can get you booted from the platform, and once you're booted, it's very hard to get back in.

Photo

Many elements of your profile are subject to Upwork verification. You are, at some point, required to take part in a brief video chat with an Upwork representative, so, if you use someone else's photo in your profile, you may very well find yourself excommunicado—not the best beginning for your freelancing career.

The first thing to catch your eye in any Upwork profile is the photo. It isn't by chance your photo occupies a prominent space. Images have impact—a significantly greater impact than text. So, it is important that you have a high resolution photo, a good background, adequate lighting, and acceptable attire.

To paraphrase Robert Burns, the national poet of Scotland, "If only we could see ourselves as others see us?" How can you be sure you have a first-rate photo? Well—there's an app for that! Photofeeler.com is a free online application that scores your photo for any of 3 uses:

- Business
- Social
- Dating

For your Upwork profile, you will want to choose business. After you upload your picture to photofeeler.com, their viewers rate it from one to ten for each of the following criteria:

- Competent
- Likable
- Influential

The service is free, and you are not limited to just one photo. You can earn views for your photos by viewing and rating other users' photos. However, if you prefer, you can purchase credits for faster test results. The website is incredibly user friendly, and it has information on how to take your own professional headshots, so try it!

Name

You must use your actual name. Upwork will require you to submit a government ID such as your passport, or driver's license. Obviously your name must match your ID.

Location

Claiming to work from a location you believe has the potential to attract a higher rate of pay is tempting. For example, if you live in India and want high paying clients from the United States, stating that you live in the U.S. may seem like a great idea. However, it is a flawed idea. There are multiple ways Upwork can find out. Time zones are one, and your IP address is another. Your IP address reveals your location, and then there is the matter of your ID. Honesty is always the best policy. Besides, you have a secret weapon, this book. It doesn't matter where you are located, after applying the principles in this book, you can charge whatever rate you want because you'll be a premium freelancer.

Job Success Score (JSS)

Upwork's *Job Success Score* is something over which you have indirect control. You earn your JSS and it only appears in your profile after you have completed a job and received a rating from the client. I will have a great deal more to share with you on this topic later in the book. For now, let's say that, although an important part of your profile, the JSS is not something that you directly control.

Badges

Badges, like your JSS, are earned. They have the potential to bring you more work, more invitations, and more money. Earn them by consistently providing a great work product to your clients. We'll talk more about badges later in the book.

Total Earnings / Hours Worked

Upwork tracks your total earnings, and hours worked. These statistics are a function of the fees clients pay you and the hours you work. However, if you only accept fixed price work, your profile will always reflect zero hours worked. As a practical matter, most freelancers work a mix of hourly and fixed price jobs.

Number of Jobs (Completed and in Progress)

Total jobs include completed jobs and jobs in progress. Upwork deems a job to be in progress until the contract ends. It is the client's responsibility to end the contract when the freelancer satisfactorily completes the job. Freelancers may end the contract in the absence of any action on the client's part. I'll take a deeper dive into this in the chapter on the JSS, but for now, this is all you need to know as it relates to your profile.

Title

Your profile's title must be very clear and succinct. It must convey exactly what you do. Use power words. Words that pack a wallop! Examples of power words include amazing, epic, thrilling, misleading, tested, ironclad, and little-known, to name just a few. Make it interesting so you get the prospect's attention and hold it. It should also intrigue, which encourages the prospect to continue reading. Make the prospect want more! Importantly, the title should emphasize the prospect's goals—not yours.

Introduction / Bio / Overview

An overview is very much like an elevator pitch, a synopsis of your work experience and background. Your overview should contain as much information as possible in the first sentence or two. When prospects browse freelancer profiles, this is what they see.

 Jacqueline R.
Experienced & Efficient Writer/Editor
United States

$85.00 / hr   **$10k+** earned   100% Job Success

Hi there, I am a freelance writer with 20+ years experience in publishing and digital content creation. My work has been published by large media outlets like Disney, NBC Universal and Common Sense Me ...

English Dialects • English - North America

Content Writing Services • Content Writing • Editing & Proofreading • Research • SEO • 2 more

3 more

It is very apparent that freelancers have but a small window of opportunity to grab the prospect's attention. Therefore, it is critical to have an impressive title, and an overview that gets quickly to the point. In short, be brief and be persuasive. I'll have more on how to do this later in the book.

Hourly Rate

Upwork freelancers are free to choose the hourly rate they wish to charge. However, it helps to know that from the prospect's perspective, hourly rates of less than $20 are entry level rates, rates of $20 to $40 are intermediate rates, and rates above $40 are expert rates. On this basis, make an honest assessment of your skill level and set your hourly rate accordingly. It would only make you look foolish to say you have intermediate skill levels and then charge an hourly rate that reflects an entry level skill set.

Video (Optional—but not really!)

Although Upwork rates your profile as complete, with or without a video, I strongly recommend including one. As mentioned earlier, I did a great deal of testing regarding my profile. I estimate that only 5 to 8 percent of freelancers include a video on their profile. Including a video puts your profile in the upper 90th percentile of all the profiles on Upwork.

My research reveals that a video can boost your click through rate substantially, as much as 31 percent. Later in the book, I'll tell you what you need to know to make a killer video that converts like gangbusters.

Availability

This setting informs potential prospects of your availability to work. The primary setting allows you to choose between available & unavailable. If you choose available, there are 3 sub-settings:

- Over 30 hrs/wk
- Less than 30 hrs/wk
- As needed—open to offers

Note: If you choose the *unavailable* setting, Upwork does not display your profile to prospects searching for freelancers.

Employment History

Record your employment history in this section, giving particular emphasis to those jobs that parallel the type of work you seek. Here is your opportunity to use keywords you want to rank for. Many freelancers skimp on the descriptions in this section. Don't skimp! A well thought out and thorough employment history will separate you from 90% of the other freelancers on the platform and the Upwork algorithms will love you for it.

Other Experiences

Take full advantage of the opportunity to share experiences you believe apply to the services you offer. This may include knowledge that you have gained through volunteer work or travel.

Languages

This setting permits you to choose your language and your level of proficiency in that language. Avoid embarrassing yourself by choosing the proficiency level that best describes your abilities.

Verifications

Account verification is the simple process of scanning and submitting a government ID, such as your driver's license or passport, to Upwork. A video chat with an Upwork staffer, usually lasting less than ten minutes, completes the verification.

Phone number verification is optional, unless specifically requested by a prospect or by Upwork.

Once verification is complete, you receive a badge beside your name, which looks like this: ⬢

Education

This is where you will list your educational achievements, especially important when a credible link exists between your academic background and the services you offer.

Testimonials (Employers Outside of Upwork) | Certifications and Awards

If you've yet to land a job (and even you have), the option to solicit testimonials from former employers outside the Upwork platform is one you should pursue. An endorsement from former employers adds value to your profile. Few freelancers take advantage of this. So, if you do, it sets you apart from the crowd.

By all means, showcase any awards or certifications relating to the services you provide your prospects.

Skills (Tags)

Freelancers may choose a maximum of ten skills to display on a profile. I recommend using the maximum number. They are easy to select via a drop-down box. Having more skills listed will get you invited to more jobs, and you'll appear in more results from companies doing searches.

I firmly believe the most successful profiles are those with the most relevant information, targeted to the prospect's needs and in line with the services you offer.

ESTABLISHING YOUR VALUE

Value-added is one of many buzzwords used in the business community, but it is an under-used tactic in the freelance community. The term's definition varies, depending on its context. In freelancing, the term means showing your value to the prospect—upfront—before you enter any formal contract.

Value-added means that you enhance the perceived value of your services. By adding value to your service, you create an incentive for the client to choose your services over the services of your competition. You accomplish this through your profile, through your proposal, and sometimes, after the contract ends.

It is critically important that you listen to your clients so you can determine what they truly value.

Add value to your service by highlighting the expertise you bring to the job, or by offering additional services at no charge. For example, if you are a writer, you might offer to include unlimited revisions, or a *no plagiarism* verification via a *Copyscape* screen shot. Even services that face tremendous competition, such as writing, can be differentiated from the competition by including a service that adds perceived value.

When you add value to your service, you will attract more clients and generate higher earnings. Here are six ways you can establish your value:

Show-off Your Pedigree

Highlight, in your profile and/or in your proposal, any special training, certifications, licenses, qualifications, or accreditations related to your niche and/or to the job for which you are applying. In short, whatever you have in your background or experience that shows you are qualified to do the job.

Endorsement from an Authority

If you have work experience with influential individuals or with a well-known person in a relevant field, get a reference. Upwork calls them *Testimonials* and you can make requests directly from your *Profile* page. Such endorsements add value to your profile and to your proposal so, be sure to mention any relevant testimonials in your proposal. While testimonials from such persons are valuable, any credible reference is a plus.

Social Validation

If you are freelancing on Upwork's platform, you are automatically receiving social validation via the *Work History* section of your profile. You can and should augment this by using the *Testimonial* feature. Always reference relevant client feedback in your proposal.

You can also use quotes from performance reviews, reference letters, or LinkedIn testimonials to use in your proposals. This is helpful for new freelancers who have yet to develop a *Work History*. Be certain to choose quotes that sound personal, authentic, and are specific to skills needed in the job. Avoid generic or bland quotes. For example, if organizational skills are important in the job, then choose a quote that speaks to that.

Value Related Keywords

Using keywords and active verbs will add value to your profile and your proposals. Examples of active verbs include such words as analyzed, advised, amended, brainstormed, boosted, budgeted, challenged, coordinated, critiqued, developed, directed, drafted, edited, eliminated, endorsed, focused, fueled, formulated, generated, graphed, grouped, helped, handled, headed, identified, implemented, induced, judged, launched, led, managed, minimized, motivated, negotiated, navigated, networked, owned, oversaw, organized, proposed, planned, pioneered, queried, qualified, quoted, resolved, rewarded, reviewed, secured, simplified, supported, trained, transformed, tested, updated, upgraded, undertook, validated, visualized, verified, weighed, wrote, and won.

Determine the keywords and key phrases you should use in your proposal by scouring the job posting. Mirror the important relevant words and phrases in your proposal. Use these keywords and phrases to show how you successfully helped other clients.

Prove Your Value through Theory/Logic

Occasionally there will be instances when you know that you are a logical fit for the job, but you don't have the credentials to prove it. In such cases, the best approach is to make your argument in a clear, simple, and straightforward manner. For example, if a client is looking for an editor to edit his self-help book, consider headlining your proposal with, "Editor with five years of experience editing self-help books." This is a simple but effective approach.

Under no circumstances am I suggesting you misrepresent yourself or your abilities. What I *am* suggesting is that you find as much commonality as possible between your experience and the prospect's needs.

Tell Your Story

Express your value by telling the story behind a similar job you successfully handled in the past. One in which your client faced comparable problems to those of your prospect. Define the problems and the solutions you put forward to resolve them.

You can do this in a narrative style or through bullet points.

For example, let's say you were asked to develop a marketing strategy for a company trapped in a niche that seemed too small to develop into a profitable enterprise.

Solutions:

- Introduced new subsites to increase traffic
- Boosted ad revenues through the addition of new sponsors
- Launched e-commerce store that generated $250,000 in revenues

Results:

- Drove a 100 percent increase in revenues by expanding the company's niche, which opened up new opportunities.

When a prospect reads your story, they can visualize how you would impact their company, resolve their problems, and capitalize on their opportunities.

Consider adding value to your client relationship, even after you have successfully completed the job. Show the client you appreciate and value their business. One way I have done this is by sending high value clients gift baskets as a gesture of my appreciation for the work. If you have just wrapped up a contract valued in the thousands, why not send a $30, $40, or $50 gift basket?

This gesture has worked well for me, and I see no reason it won't work for you. I have found that sending clients gift baskets increase my earnings by 22 percent. These clients stay with me an average of 3.5 months longer. These two factors more than offset the expense.

If you decide to try this, don't be cheap! Just Google *corporate gift baskets* and choose a reputable firm. This is a great way to strengthen client relationships!

DETERMINE HOW YOU WANT TO CHARGE

Earlier in the book, I went into detail regarding the factors involved in determining your hourly rate. However, many jobs on Upwork are fixed price, not hourly. Be assured, you haven't wasted your time. You will use the hourly rate, over which you labored so intensely, as a benchmark to arrive at a fixed price in your proposal.

Expert Content Writer To Prepare A Content Brief

Fixed-price - Expert - Est. Budget: $10 - Posted 9 minutes ago

I am looking for a content planner to prepare a brief for an article topic.

I am hoping this will turn to a long-term contract soo.

You must be a Native English speaker.

I will pay $10/brief.

I will send a sample of what I want to the most qualified.

Thank you. less

Content Writing   Editing & Proofreading   Research   English

Proposals: **Less than 5**

Payment verified   ★★★★★   **$900+** spent   📍 United States

56

For example, in the above job posting, you will see the line immediately below the job description provides you with valuable information.

- It defines the job as being fixed price,
- They require an expert level freelancer,
- The client expects to pay $10 for the completed job.

To determine whether to apply for this job, you must ask yourself:

1.] Am I an *expert* and have I identified myself as an *expert* in my profile?

2.] Does my hourly rate reflect the value an *expert* would place on his/her time?

3.] How long will it take to complete the job as described?

If your answer to numbers 1 and 2 is yes, then you must estimate the time you will need to complete the project. Personally, I believe the minimum time needed to accomplish any job, however small, is 30 minutes. If you determine this job will take one-half hour to complete, and your rate is $35/hour, you will need compensation in the amount of $17.50 for the job described. However, the prospect's budget is $10, so should you submit a proposal?

Probably not, but let's dig deeper and look at the prospect's feedback.

I have selected three fixed price job reviews for similar work that reveal information key to your decision whether to apply. First, we see that *Hannah I.* has been selected on two previous occasions for similar work, and received five-star reviews. This begs the question; will *Hannah I.* be invited to this job? Second, you see that the prospect routinely pays freelancers at a rate below your expected rate of compensation. At this point, you can decide. I would not apply to this posting. What would your decision be?

As you know, you can filter your job search. You can choose one of three options shown below.

Job Type

- ☑ Any Job Type
- ☐ Hourly (19,232)
- ☐ Fixed Price (14,358)

The question of how you want to charge (by the hour or fixed price) needs to be addressed. If you search for jobs that only pay by the hour, you are leaving a lot of potential work (and money) on the table and vice versa. To illustrate this, I created the chart below. Let me be clear—these results were based on data for a single day. It is a snapshot, not an exhaustive research project.

On that day, almost 36 percent of jobs were fixed price jobs, while 64 percent were hourly rate jobs. If you were only accepting hourly jobs on that day, you would have left over one-third of all potential jobs on the table.

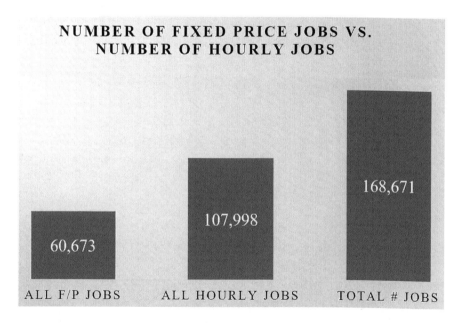

NUMBER OF FIXED PRICE JOBS VS. NUMBER OF HOURLY JOBS

Let's look at the pros and cons of fixed price jobs.

Pros

- Broadly, fixed price jobs are easier to land.

- Because fixed price jobs are more likely to have a rapid turnaround compared to hourly jobs, freelancers, especially newbies, can quickly build a *Work History*, which is important because it is the principal driver of your JSS.

- Fixed price jobs usually pay faster than do hourly rate jobs, with funds being available as soon as five days after client approval. Upwork bases hourly jobs on a weekly billing cycle, Monday through Sunday, and releases payment for the hours worked during the billing cycle ten days after the billing cycle ends.

- Since fixed price jobs are usually completed quickly compared to hourly jobs, you can complete more jobs, which not only provides you with enhanced potential to gain experience and learn new skills, it also increases your activity level on the platform.

Cons

- Although funds can be available in as few as 5 days, clients have up to 14 days to review and approve the release of funds.

- While positive reviews can be achieved rapidly through fixed price jobs, negative reviews can escalate just as quickly. You must never lose sight of the fact that a negative review risk is associated with any contract.

- Reviews for fixed price work typically exert less of an impact on your JSS than do long-term, hourly contracts because fixed price contracts are usually worth less. The larger the value of the contract, the greater the impact on your JSS. However, all ratings and comments *are* visually impactful. The client's eyes are drawn to 5-stars and positive comments first, and then to the value of the contract, if at all.

- No matter how careful you are, it is difficult, from a net earnings standpoint, to win with fixed price contracts. Unless you are very experienced and have a very clear scope of work, it usually works out that the hours you spend completing the job do not line up favorably with your hourly rate. In short, most freelancers underestimate the time needed to complete the job. This could result from your miscalculation or the client's failure to define the project's scope—or a combination of these.

- High fees are another issue with fixed price jobs since these jobs rarely exceed the $500 threshold necessary to avoid the 20 percent fee. Again, let me be clear—the results displayed in the chart below were based on data for a single day. It is a snapshot, not an exhaustive research project. On that day, of all available Upwork fixed price jobs, just under 25 percent had a budget greater than $500. Please understand, there will be variations in these percentages from niche to niche, and day to day. The point is that fixed price jobs valued over $500 are a fraction of the total number of fixed prices jobs.

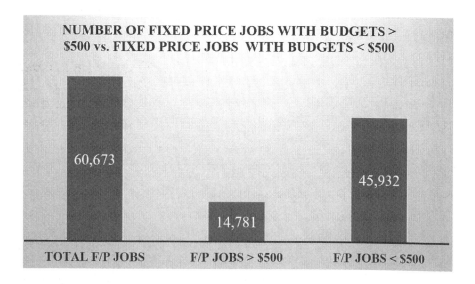

- On the day represented by the above graph, you would have had a 1 in 4 chance of avoiding Upwork's 20 percent fee on a fixed price job (see chart below).

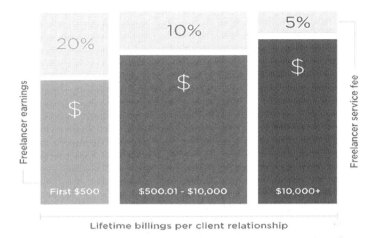

Lifetime billings per client relationship

- Repeat hires by the same client are a potential workaround, but do you want to bank on that possibility?

Most fixed price jobs will fall into the first bucket. If you do several fixed price jobs with a budget of less than $500 that total $1500, you will pay $300 in fees. Conversely, if you land one hourly job for $850, and another for $650, you will pay only $150 in fees—one-half of your fee expense on fixed price jobs.

Hourly contracts also have pros & cons, which are discussed below.

Pros

- Hourly rate contracts are almost always more interesting than fixed price contracts because their scope is broader, often representing the entire project, while fixed price jobs are often a small part of a larger project. For example, an hourly job editing an entire book, vs. a fixed price editing job for one chapter. I think everyone would agree that it is easier to avoid burn-out if you involve yourself in interesting, even challenging work.

- You are much more likely to build long-term relationships with hourly rate clients than fixed price clients. Over a longer term, trust, perhaps friendship, can blossom between client and freelancer, which is not a bad outcome in the lonely world of freelancing.

- Sustainability is an important goal for any business and a difficult one to achieve as a freelancer. However, by grooming a loyal following of hourly rate clients (I call them *anchor* clients), sustainability is achievable and relieves you from the stress of seeking a constant stream of new clients.

- Hourly and fixed price contracts both provide you with the opportunity to upsell additional services, however the longer-term client relationship, inherent in hourly contracts, gives it the edge.

Cons

- Hourly contracts can be more difficult to land, from a time standpoint. Even if you have an interview with the prospect, it is probably one of several the prospect is conducting, making it several days or longer before the prospect decides.

- Fixed price jobs are typically well-defined and leave little doubt regarding client expectations in terms of deliverables, while hourly rate jobs are less well-defined. Often, for hourly jobs, it is more difficult to gain a complete understanding of what the client expects compared to fixed rate jobs, and what they *expect* will usually evolve over the course of the contract. This can be unsettling.

The fact is, as you begin your freelance journey, you will be so hungry that your instinct will be to eat everything on the table. I can't tell you what course to chart, but I can show you how to best reach your destination of sustainable, interesting, and plentiful work.

USE THE SKYSCRAPER TECHNIQUE TO JUMPSTART YOUR CREATIVITY

Inspiration can be scarce sometimes. A writer might refer to this situation as writer's block, an artist may say they are experiencing creative block, or an athlete may acknowledge that he has fallen into a slump.

The skyscraper technique is a useful method to kick-start your imagination and find inspiration by using someone else's written word as a jumping off point, make it your own and make it unique to you. It is an effective technique to use on your competition.

In the examples that follow, I will show you how to use the profiles of your competitors to gain inspiration for your profile. In this example, I am choosing the proofreading niche.

Begin the process at the Upwork menu bar. Click on the white triangle to reveal the drop-down box. Then highlight talent.

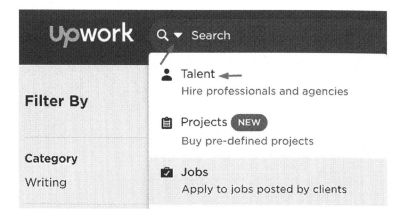

After that you will see a screen that looks similar to this:

You will want to choose freelancers in your niche (competitors), so select the writing category. Once that is selected, click on the green arrow (upper-right) and select *Editing & Proofreading* from the drop-down menu.

Begin browsing the profiles until you see something that inspires you.

Claudia E.
Elite Editor/Proofreader
United States

$40.00 / hr   **$100+** earned

I re-write your wrongs. I proof you perform. Let me make your good writing better. With four years of experience in the English language field, you can be confident in my mastery of Lexicon. Working a ...

Editing & Proofreading Services • Copyediting

After browsing 110 profiles in this niche, I found the two examples above that provide me with inspiration. In the first example, I found inspiration in the frank approach and the clever reference to Dr. Frankenstein. The second example offers a play on words that captures my attention.

If I were freelancing in the *Editing & Proofreading* niche, I would have no trouble building on these ideas. That's skyscraping!

To be clear, unlike plagiarism, skyscraping is all about finding inspiration and using that inspiration to create something uniquely your own. Plagiarism, on the other hand, is the act of copying another person's work, word-for-word, without attribution and without quotation marks. That *is not* skyscraping!

AGGREGATED LISTENING TECHNIQUE

You are, no doubt, acquainted with the old saying, "There's more than one way to skin a cat." Well, the tip I'm sharing with you in this chapter has nothing to do with cats, but *everything* to do with another way of finding jobs on Upwork. The old-fashioned method is to log into Upwork, go to *Find Work*, create and/or apply your search and browse the jobs.

All this takes time, and your time is valuable. If you could bypass those time-consuming steps, would you? If you could receive those Upwork jobs in your email account instead of checking *Find Work* multiple times during the day, would you? Sure you would!

You can accomplish this in two simple steps, 1) sign up for a free RSS feed reader, and 2) activate your Upwork RSS feed. Personally, I use *Blogtrottr*. It is free, and user friendly, however, there are dozens of such applications available on the Internet, such as *NewsFlow*, *RSSOwl*, and *Omea Reader* to name a few. Just Google *free RSS reader* and browse your options.

Upwork offers two options for activating your RSS feed. Once you log in, click on *Find Work* in the menu bar.

This brings up *My Feed* and your first opportunity to select your RSS feed as shown below. In this example, you click on the 3 dots inside the circle.

My Feed

This activates the drop-down box from which you select RSS, which is a widely used feed format. The *Atom* feed is an RSS alternative, meeting Internet Engineering Task Force (IETF) standards. The only significant difference between the two is that RSS provides either plain text or escaped HTML as formats, while Atom can feed in a broader variety of formats. For this task, RSS is the better choice in my opinion.

Your second option is to select a feed based upon one of the *saved searches* you have created. When you select a saved search, you'll see a small green icon immediately to the right. Click this to open your saved search.

Then you will see this icon. Click it and select RSS.

Regardless of the icon used, when you click on RSS it brings up this screen of gobbledygook you see below. Don't worry about the gobbledygook. Just copy the URL and paste it into Blogtrottr or whatever RSS reader you have selected.

All that remains for you to do is to create a folder for the feeds sent to your email. In the example below, the freelancer has created a sub-folder in their Gmail account for the emails generated by the feed. If you wish, you can create a filter that automatically directs these emails into the sub-folder.

I call this technique *aggregated listening*! It will save you gobs of time and improve the speed at which you learn about jobs that perfectly fit your skill set, which translates into more jobs for you.

Occasionally Blogtrottr has an issue with long URLs and returns an error message. If this happens, you can solve the problem by pasting the URL into Bitly.com or a similar link shortener. Then paste the resulting shortened link into Blogtrottr. This should resolve the problem.

Now, given all of the above, there is an easier way to get instant alerts not just from Upwork but from many other top freelancing sites. Go to Vollna.com and open an account. With Vollna, you simply enter a few pieces of information of the type of jobs you are looking for, set your alert and Vollna sends off matches. What's great about Vollna is you can see important stats on how many times you are hired vs how many times you applied for jobs. Knowing this is critical to your success if you have specific goals. For example, if you know that for every 10 jobs you apply to that you will be hired for 2 of them, and that your average customer is worth $5000, then you know that for every 10 jobs you apply to that you will receive $10,000 (2 X $5,000). Check out Vollna, I use it, and you should too.

HOW TO CREATE YOUR UPWORK PROFILE AND AVOID AMATEURISH MISTAKES

You have been creating the information for your profile from the moment of your birth. Everything you've learned, every class you've taken, every job you've held, every life experience you've had—all these, and more—could impact your Upwork profile. That's why every freelancer's profile is unique, just as each individual is unique.

As you go through life, you will have new experiences, and gain new skills, which will alter your profile. This is important to remember. Your Upwork profile isn't written in stone. You can edit and alter it to reflect fresh experiences and new skills. Your profile is not a once-and-done proposition. It requires constant attention because *you* are constantly changing. Fortunately, Upwork allows you to edit your profile. Understanding that changes to your profile are possible should relieve any stress you are feeling about creating your profile.

Although I can't create your profile, I can tell you *how* to create your profile. Think of your profile as a picture puzzle, a puzzle with nineteen pieces. These pieces must fit together perfectly to create the overall picture. Each piece has its role to play, and if you force just one piece of the puzzle into a place where it doesn't belong, the picture will be corrupted.

Earlier in this section, you read the chapter *Nineteen Elements that Make Your Upwork Profile Rock.* These elements are the pieces of the puzzle that make up your profile. Let's look at them again.

1.] Photo

2.] Name

3.] Location

4.] Job Success Score (JSS)

5.] Badges

6.] Total Earnings / Hours Worked

7.] Number of Jobs (*Completed* and *In Progress*)

8.] Title

9.] Introduction / Bio / Overview

10.] Hourly Rate

11.] Video (Optional)

12.] Availability

13.] Employment History

14.] Other Experiences

15.] Languages

16.] Verifications

17.] Education

18.] Testimonials (Employers outside of Upwork) | Certifications and Awards

19.] Skills (Tags)

Creating a basic profile need not be a daunting task. Many of the puzzle pieces are self-resolving, meaning you have no direct input. These include Job Success Score, Badges, Total Earnings/Hours Worked, Number of Jobs (*Completed* and *In Progress*), and Verifications.

With these eliminated, only 14 remain. Of these 14, three are straightforward and require no thought or preparation. They are Name, Location, and Languages. That leaves only 11 profile puzzle pieces which require careful thought and thorough preparation, and one of these 11, the

Video, is optional. However, I would definitely recommend that you include a video because it has a measurable impact on rankings. I've already addressed what you need to know on this subject in *Making a Killer Video*, found in the *Convert* section so jump ahead and use that information to create your video. That leaves ten remaining puzzle pieces, and the rest of this chapter will focus on those.

Launching your Upwork profile is a simple task if you do all the prep work beforehand. For example, you should complete your Title, and Introduction / Bio / Overview in MS Word or similar software. This will give you complete flexibility to edit, spellcheck, and perfect the text. Then, when complete, just copy & paste into your profile.

I've already addressed what you need to know regarding these elements below in the chapter *Nineteen Elements that Make Your Upwork Profile Rock*. I understand that toggling back to an earlier chapter can be frustrating as you work on completing your profile, so I have duplicated my remarks below. Hopefully, this not only makes it easier for you but also ensures that you overlook nothing.

Photo

Many elements of your profile are subject to Upwork verification. You are, at some point, required to take part in a brief video chat with an Upwork representative, so, if you use someone else's photo in your profile, you may very well find yourself excommunicado—not the best beginning for your freelancing career.

The first thing to catch your eye in any Upwork profile is the photo. It isn't by chance your photo occupies a prominent space. Images have impact—a significantly greater impact than text. So, it is important that you have a high resolution photo, a good background, adequate lighting, and acceptable attire.

To paraphrase Robert Burns, the national poet of Scotland, "If only we could see ourselves as others see us?" How can you be sure you have a first-rate photo? Well—there's an app for that! Photofeeler.com is a free online application that scores your photo for any of 3 uses:

- Business
- Social
- Dating

For your Upwork profile, you will want to choose business. After you upload your picture to photofeeler.com, their viewers rate it from one to ten for each of the following criteria:

- Competent
- Likable
- Influential

The service is free, and you are not limited to just one photo. You can earn views for your photos by viewing and rating other users' photos. However, if you prefer, you can purchase credits for faster test results. The website is incredibly user friendly, and it has information on how to take your own professional headshots, so try it!

Title

Your profile's title must be very clear and succinct. It must convey exactly what you do. Use power words. Words that pack a wallop! Examples of power words include amazing, epic, thrilling, misleading, tested, ironclad, and little-known, to name just a few. Make it interesting so you get the prospect's attention and hold it. It should also intrigue, which encourages the prospect to continue reading. Make the prospect want more! Importantly, the title should emphasize the prospect's goals—not yours.

Introduction / Bio / Overview

An overview is very much like an elevator pitch, a synopsis of your work experience and background. Your overview should contain as much information as possible in the first sentence or two. When prospects browse freelancer profiles, this is what they see.

Jacqueline R.
Experienced & Efficient Writer/Editor
United States

$85.00 / hr   **$10k+** earned   100% Job Success

Hi there, I am a freelance writer with 20+ years experience in publishing and digital content creation. My work has been published by large media outlets like Disney, NBC Universal and Common Sense Me ...

English Dialects • English - North America

Content Writing Services • Content Writing • Editing & Proofreading • Research • SEO • 2 more

3 more

It is very apparent that freelancers have but a small window of opportunity to grab the prospect's attention. Therefore, it is critical to have an impressive title, and an overview that gets quickly to the point. In short, be brief and be persuasive. I'll have more on how to do this later in the book.

Hourly Rate

Upwork freelancers are free to choose the hourly rate they wish to charge. However, it helps to know that from the prospect's perspective, hourly rates of less than $20 are entry level rates, rates of $20 to $40 are intermediate rates, and rates above $40 are expert rates. On this basis, make an honest assessment of your skill level and set your hourly rate accordingly. It would only make you look foolish to say you have intermediate skill levels and then charge an hourly rate that reflects an entry level skill set.

Availability

This setting informs potential prospects of your availability to work. The primary setting allows you to choose between available & unavailable. If you choose available, there are 3 sub-settings:

- Over 30 hrs/wk
- Less than 30 hrs/wk
- As needed—open to offers

Note: If you choose the *unavailable* setting, Upwork does not display your profile to prospects searching for freelancers.

Employment History

Record your employment history in this section, giving particular emphasis to those jobs that parallel the type of work you seek. Here is your opportunity to use keywords you want to rank for. Many freelancers skimp on the descriptions in this section. Don't skimp! A well thought out and thorough employment history will separate you from 90% of the other freelancers on the platform and the Upwork algorithms will love you for it.

Other Experiences

Take full advantage of the opportunity to share experiences you believe apply to the services you offer. This may include knowledge that you have gained through volunteer work or travel.

Education

This is where you will list your educational achievements. It is especially important when a credible link exists between your educational background and the services you offer.

Testimonials (Employers outside of Upwork) | Certifications and Awards

If you've yet to land a job (and even you have), the option to solicit testimonials from former employers outside the Upwork platform is one you should pursue. An endorsement from former employers adds value to your profile. Few freelancers take advantage of this. So, if you do, it sets you apart from the crowd.

By all means, showcase any awards or certifications relating to the services you provide your prospects.

Skills (Tags)

Freelancers may choose a maximum of ten skills to display on a profile. I recommend using the maximum number. They are easy to select via a drop-down box. Having more skills listed will get you invited to more jobs, and you'll appear in more results from companies doing searches.

What I've shared with you in this chapter will allow you to hit the ground running as you begin your freelance career. However, it is only a beginning. In the next chapter, I'll show you how to build on the foundation you've just laid and take your profile to even greater heights!

HOW TO BUILD AN OPTIMIZED PROFILE, GET NOTICED, AND EARN WHAT YOU'RE WORTH

In my experience, the success of your Upwork profile depends entirely on a thorough understanding of the interplay between the elements involved. Your profile's success or failure turns on three factors—the skills, experiences, and expertise you bring to the table, a thorough understanding of what your prospects need, and, too often overlooked, what Upwork needs. Yes. What Upwork needs!

As an Upwork freelancer, you need to please not only your clients but also Upwork. Early in the book you read *Understanding the Algorithm*. It is no accident that this is one of the longest chapters of the book. In this chapter you learned the factors Upwork deems important to the success of its business model. Since Upwork's success and yours go arm in arm, I urge you to re-read this chapter before optimizing your profile.

If you want to know if you are pleasing Upwork, just go to your *My Stats* page. This can be found in the drop-down menu under *Find Work*. Upwork's algorithm is rather complex, and I won't pretend that the *My Stats* page is all-encompassing, however, it is the best insight available to you as an Upwork freelancer. Ignore it at your peril.

In the previous chapter, *How to Create Your First Upwork Profile and Avoid Amateurish Mistakes*, I've covered the nineteen elements of the Upwork profile. In this chapter, it is my aim to concentrate on those elements which can be optimized, taken to a higher level, and improved in order to make your profile stand out. After all, the purpose of your profile is to attract the attention of prospects. If you cannot gain their attention, how can you earn?

Below are the elements I have selected as the foremost candidates for optimization:

Photo

As I've said many times, a great profile picture is priority #1, #2, and #3. Kick it up a few notches! Is it taken with an HD camera? Is the background free of distractions? Are you dressed your best? Are you well-groomed, smiling, leaning forward, looking open and friendly? Have you used photofeeler. com to assist in your selection? Is the lighting acceptable? If your answer to any of these is no, then optimize your photo.

Job Success Score (JSS)

At this juncture in your freelance career, you are no longer a newbie. What level of job success is reflected in your score? If you have ten jobs under your belt and only three clients liked your work, that nets you a JSS of 30 percent. You know full well that you must have a JSS of 90 percent and above to compete successfully on Upwork's platform. You must optimize your JSS! Review the chapters, *All about the Job Success Score (JSS)* and *Recovering from a Bad JSS*.

Badges

Badges are a function of your JSS. If you haven't earned one, re-read *All About Badges*. You will need to optimize your JSS in order to earn a badge.

Total Earnings / Hours Worked

Having progressed beyond the newbie stage, it is important that you grow your *Total Earnings* and *Hours Worked* stats. Prospects can filter based on these statistics, so optimizing your profile means growing these numbers. Until you do so, your profile may never cross their gaze.

Number of Jobs (*Completed and In Progress*)

This is not a filterable parameter, but it is an important one from a prospect's perspective. The more completed jobs your profile reflects, the greater the prospect's confidence in hiring you will be (and the happier Upwork will be). If you have a JSS below 90 percent, optimize your portfolio by increasing successful job completions.

In Progress jobs frequently reflect long-term clients. Long term clients are clients that have worked with you consistently for a period of 3 months or more. They may be long-term hourly jobs or fixed price jobs with milestones or a combination of both. Having a 25 percent or higher percentage is a factor that will boost your JSS. If you are not there, optimize!

Long-term clients ➤ **27%**

Title

Your title is extremely important to your click through rate (views), second only to your photo, or arguably tied for first. Once again, I direct you to the *My Stats* page. If your profile is not being discovered—that's an issue. If your profile isn't discovered, you aren't getting invitations.

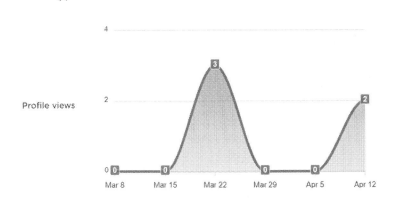

Your profile was discovered **2 times** last week.

A low discovery number means that you need to optimize! A title needs to entice the prospect and convince the prospect to take a deeper look. Does your title describe exactly what you do? For example, does your title read *Article Writer*, when it should read *Compelling Article Writer for High Traffic Blog Sites?*

Beyond enticing, a title must reveal **exactly** what you do. It must use words that pack a wallop (power words), and it should focus on meeting your prospective clients' goals, not *your* goals.

I've spoken often about testing titles. Don't be bashful about changing up your title if it isn't creating the desired results—one change at a time, please. Since we are not all talented writers, consider hiring a freelance copywriter to assist you in perfecting your title (and overview). It may prove to be money well spent!

Introduction / Bio / Overview

A freelancer's overview shares many characteristics and functions of the title. They work in concert, so any disconnect will cause a problem. An overview must be succinct and get to the point immediately. Powerful, descriptive words are just as important to your overview as they are to your title.

As you know, prospects browsing your profile see only the first couple of sentences. You must craft these opening sentences in such a way that the prospect is inspired to click on the preview and learn more about you.

Testing is important! If your overview falls short of your expectations, make integral changes. Document the results and, if need be, try something else. One change at a time! You've heard the adage, "You have to spend money to make money." There is no shame in getting expert help with your overview and title. Hire a copywriter—on Upwork's platform, of course!

If you aren't getting the results you need, don't ignore the problem hoping it will go away. Be proactive—optimize!

Hourly Rate

Hourly rates are rarely an issue with rankings. However, inconsistencies must be avoided. For example, if your hourly rate is entry level (less than $20/hour) and you are expecting intermediate or expert jobs—that will not happen. Optimizing your profile's hourly rate means ensuring that your skill set, background, JSS and client reviews support the hourly rate your profile reflects. If not, change it!

Video (Optional)

Upwork suggests that a video is optional. From my perspective, it isn't. A quality video makes your profile stand out. If you don't already have a video, create one! I have tested the effects of a video on click-through rates extensively. A video will increase your click through rate by as much as 31 percent and put our profile in the 90th percentile of profiles on Upwork's platform.

If you have a video, but aren't getting the results you expected (YouTube shows the number of views) then consider optimizing your video.

Use a better camera, ensure there are no lighting issues such as shadows or glare, make sure there is no distracting background noise and that your voice is clear. How's your background? Are there distractions, such as clutter, or someone wandering through your camera's field of vision?

How is your delivery? Do you capture the viewer's attention in the opening few seconds? Is your delivery natural, or does it seem overly rehearsed and formal?

Are you telling a great story that creates an emotional connection with your prospect? Does your video include a call to action? Have you over-delivered?

If your answer is no, on any of these points, then you need to optimize! I suggest you begin by re-reading *Making a Killer Video*.

Employment History

Are you using your employment history to emphasize your skills? How closely does your employment history match what you offer to do for prospects? Not so much? Then you need to optimize!

Other Experiences

Have you taken full advantage of the opportunity to showcase life experiences related to your work? If not—optimize!

Education

Is your focus in this section to highlight how your academic credentials support the work you do? If your answer is no, then you must optimize.

Testimonials (Employers outside of Upwork) | Certifications and Awards

This is one area of the profile that freelancers often neglect. Have you reached out to former employers for a testimonial? Have you added relevant certifications and awards? If not, why not? If you don't have any certificates or awards, are you planning to earn them? Being proactive is key to your success. Adopt a mindset of continuous improvement. If you are out of groceries at home, do you just sit and starve? Of course not. So please explain why you sit on your hands when the work isn't coming in? Do something!

Skills (Tags)

Review your skill tags. Do they align with the work you are offering to do for prospects? Skills are searchable! You are allowed ten, so make sure you use all ten!

If your skill tags are out of kilter with the work you do, or if you haven't used all ten, then optimize!

Look, I've said it before and I'll say it again, your profile isn't a once-and-done affair. As you change, so must your profile. Without exaggeration, I update/change my profile at least twice a month.

You can't really lay claim to an optimized profile until you've created a *Specialized Profile*. If you've been staring at that banner for weeks on end, wondering if a *Specialized Profile* is worth the aggravation, if it delivers on its promise, if it's going to be a hassle, let me assure you it is worth your time, it delivers, and it's easy to do!

Better market your expertise with specialized profiles

Specialized profiles allow you to display more specific skills, deliverables, and more – and help power better search results and job recommendations. Learn more

Create a Specialized Profile

You may choose to create a new *Specialized Profile* or to create one using your general profile as the basis for your *Specialized Profile*. Using your existing general profile, although the easier path, defeats the purpose and spirit of having a *Specialized Profile* in my view.

One advantage of using the *Specialized Profile* is the ability to add multiple skills, whereas your regular *Profile* limits you to just ten.

Freelancers can, and should, be creative in completing step #3, *Describe your specialty*. Employ what you have learned in *Use the Skyscraper Technique on Your Competition, How to Create Your First Upwork Profile and Avoid Amateurish Mistakes*, and what you have learned in this chapter.

Just as with your general profile, you can return to it, make revisions or delete it entirely. Upwork has given freelancers a high level of control over their *Specialized Profile*. It is an exciting feature—use it—test it; benefit from it!

Oh, another advantage of having a *Specialized Profile* that no freelancer should overlook is that it offers you the ability to create a *Portfolio* to showcase your best work.

I'm an Army Veteran, but I have the utmost respect for the unofficial mantra of the Marine Corps—improvise, adapt, and overcome.

USING THE PROJECT CATALOG FEATURE

The *Project Catalog* is a relatively new offering from Upwork. It represents a host of benefits for freelancers and a substantial convenience for clients.

Client Benefits

- Clients can find exactly what they need without having to endure the hassle of posting projects and reviewing proposals.

- The *Project Catalog* dramatically shortens the time clients must invest in getting a project off the ground.

Freelancer Benefits

- Fewer hours spent pouring over job descriptions.

- Tedious proposal write-ups may be a relic of the past.

- Eliminates struggles with pricing considerations.

- No more stressful negotiating sessions.

- Jobs sourced through the *Project Catalog* do not use *Connects*.

Freelancer's will pay Upwork fees on the same basis as a fixed price project, 20 percent for projects priced at less than $500.

Upwork is investing mightily in marketing this service through press releases, social media platforms, and other media channels. With this level of investment, freelancer job opportunities have the potential to soar, so freelancers should get onboard with the *Project Catalog* program as soon as possible. Earnings may skyrocket! I'll walk you through the basics of setting up a project.

From the menu bar, go to *Find Work* and select *Profile* from the dropdown box. Scroll to down until you see *Your Project Catalog*, then click on *Manage Projects*.

That brings up the *Create Project* page. You will see this blurb just below the Menu Bar...

I strongly suggest that you browse through several projects posted by other freelancers to get a feel for this new service before attempting to create your own project. The screenshot below shows you how to get to these projects (use your client account to see these).

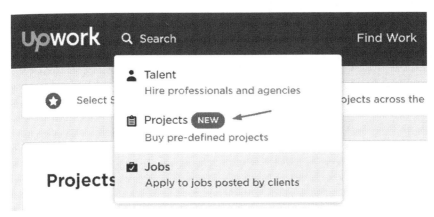

Having browsed the projects in your niche and, after using the skyscraper technique for inspiration, you are ready to create your project. Click the *Create Project* button.

That brings you to this page, where you click on *Create Project*.

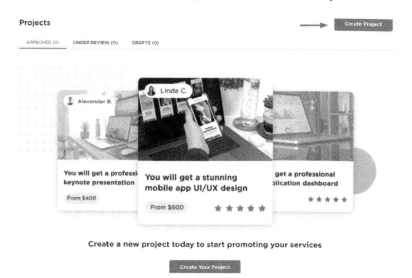

This brings you to:

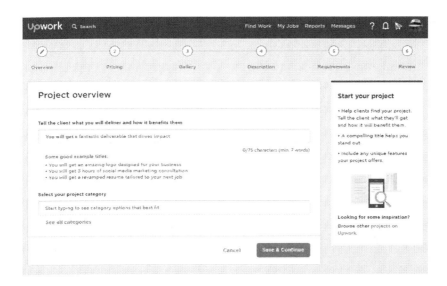

Then it's just a matter of completing each of the seven steps outlined below the Upwork menu bar. Upwork's instructions are straightforward and easy to follow so I won't take you through each of the seven steps. What I will do is provide you with some tips on maximizing your exposure.

Images

Once you've created your first project, you will undoubtedly decide to create other projects. With this in mind, it is valuable to use the *Project Catalog* as an opportunity to create your brand by using a consistent theme and photo. As you build a client base, your clients will become familiar with your theme and photo, placing them in a position to choose you for future products. Consider using canva.com or unsplash.com to create or find images that best represent your offer.

Communicate

Your project's title is of primary importance. It must convey, clearly and concisely, what the client will get when selecting your service. Upwork's project template begins every freelancer's project title with the following three words: *You will get*. This is followed by an example which you must overwrite in your own words.

Upwork allows a maximum of 75 characters in the title and you must have a minimum of 7 words. As I said—concise!

Spying AKA the Skyscraper Technique

It's important to have a grasp on what your competition is offering. As I mentioned earlier, browsing other freelancers' projects is crucial and also provides the opportunity for you to gather inspiration for your own project. Build on the ideas of your competitors and make them uniquely yours.

Specificity

The more specific you are the better. The *Project Summary* allows a maximum of 1200 characters (120 character minimum), which all but forces you to be specific. Target a specific industry or other demographic. I like to use the analogy of spearing a fish as opposed to casting a net. When going spearfishing you are looking for a very specific type of fish and have the proper tool to capture it. When casting a net however, you're not sure what type of fish you're going to pull up. Remember, specificity is the key!

UNDERSTANDING THE ALGORITHM

My testing reveals 30 factors that can affect the quality of your profile's visibility. How I came to these conclusions could be another book in its entirety, so I'll leave the details out. I spent years (and still do) testing many aspects of the algorithm, meticulously logging search results with each change of my profile. Of course, Upwork shares its algorithm with no one, but I am convinced that these factors cover 95 to 98 percent of how your profile appears in search results. The factors listed below determine how your profile ranks when clients search for freelancers on Upwork.

Profile completeness

Having a 100 percent complete profile is an absolute must. You can verify that your profile is 100 percent complete by reviewing the *My Stats* page, which appears in the drop-down box under the Find Work tab. You cannot achieve a 100 percent complete rating without a profile photo—it's so important that I have an expanded section on creating your profile photo later in the book!

Availability

Verify your availability by clicking the *Profile* tab in the *Find Work* drop-box. In the upper right-hand corner of your profile you will see a *Profile Settings* box highlighted in green. Click on this and choose *Public*. If your setting is *Private*, your profile will not appear in client searches. Next, return to the *Profile* screen and scroll down to *Availability*. Click the pencil icon and select *Available*. While you are on this screen, select one of the three options listed, 1) More than 30 hrs/week, 2) Less than 30 hrs/week, and 3) As needed - Open to offers. Clients can filter on these three options, so let's look at these from a client perspective before making a selection.

You should know the *As needed - Open to offers* option is a relatively recent replacement for a previous option, <10 hours/wk. Clients who have been on the Upwork platform for some time may view this option as having a similar meaning. Clients looking for freelancers may view the *As needed - Open to offers* setting as one used by freelancers just looking for extra income—a side hustle. Freelancers choosing the *Less than 30 hrs/week* option could be perceived as part-timers and not committed to freelancing for their principal livelihood. By indicating *More than 30 hrs/week,* you are more apt to be viewed by clients as a professional freelancer—dependent on freelancing as your sole source of income. I recommend that you make your choice based upon the client's perceptions.

Video

Having or not having a video will not affect your profile completeness percentage. However, my testing shows that a video produces a greater than 30 percent increase in visibility. Based on this statistic, you *need* a video. Keep it short, under 3 minutes, shoot the video in HD with a good camera, have a good background, and dress professionally. *Do not* script the video. It is best to work from bullet points, otherwise the result may be stilted. I will address this in greater detail later in the book.

Status (badge)

The status badge speaks to your overall performance as a freelancer. If you have earned a badge, it will appear to the right of your *Job Success Score*, and below your name. The 3 most common badges are *Rising Talent, Top Rated,* and *Top Rated Plus* There is a fourth badge, *Expert-Vetted,* held by the top 1 percent of Upwork freelancers, and offered by invitation only. It represents freelancers and agencies pre-screened by Upwork's Talent Managers for a high level of expertise and excellent soft skills.

Upwork reserves the *Rising Talent* badge for new freelancers they consider being the best new members on their platform. They qualify by completing their jobs on time and as promised, maintaining a 100 percent complete profile that accurately showcases their skills, regularly submitting proposals on jobs that match their skill set, adhering to Upwork's *Terms of Service* (TOS) and remaining active for 90 days, or have joined Upwork in the past thirty days. When Rising Talent badge-holders earn a work history, the badge will be replaced with a *Job Success Score* (JSS).

To qualify for the *Top Rated* badge, you must have a 100 percent complete profile, maintain your *Rising Talent* and/or a *JSS* of at least 90 percent for 13 of the previous 16 weeks, show a minimum 12-month earnings of $1000, have an Upwork hire that is at least ninety days old, maintain your *Available* status, be in good standing (no account holds), and have a record of activity on the platform such as proposals, invitations, and/or earnings over the past 90 days.

Earning the *Top Rated Plus* badge requires that you hold a *Top Rated* badge, earned over $10,000 in the past 12-month period, and worked on at least one large contract in the preceding 12 months. The definition of a large contract is specific to the contract's category. Certain categories may have a $5000 minimum value to qualify, while other categories may range as high as $30,000 to meet the large contract definition.

12-month earnings

This reflects the money you have earned in the previous 12 months. These are gross earnings before Upwork deducts its fees. These earnings appear in your *My Stats* page and should not be confused with lifetime earnings, which appear in your *Profile*.

Client recommended

When a contract ends, Upwork asks clients for *private* feedback as to whether they would recommend you as a freelancer. Clients rate the freelancer from one to ten, with ten being the best possible score. This differs from the *public* rating, which is expressed by the familiar one to five-star rating that appears in your profile. Conceivably, a client could give you a 5-star *public* rating but a lower rating in his *private* feedback to Upwork. The statistic that reflects the overall *private* feedback of your clients is shown as a percentage on the *My Stats* page, just to the right of the statement," Clients who would recommend you." Unless clients share this information with you, you will never know their private feedback to Upwork.

How much weight private feedback has on the algorithm is not something I wanted to experiment with, but because it absolutely affects your ability to rank well in searches, maintaining a high percentage is vital. I recommend that you work closely with your clients to ensure their total satisfaction before the contract ends.

Client retention

Keeping a client is accomplished by grooming clients capable of providing you work for a period of at least 3 months. I am not clear on how much weight client retention carries with regard to your ranking, but it has an effect. Upwork wants freelancers who can keep clients. Upwork knows which projects are long term, it is part of the job creation questionnaire, so Upwork sees both sides of the equation. Therefore, it is safe to assume that freelancers with the capacity to keep clients would have a greater likelihood of being matched with long-term projects. However, I cannot test the weight this holds on the algorithm because Upwork doesn't display the long-term client percentage on the freelancer profile.

My best guess would be that Upwork would want to see about a 20% long-term client ratio. Hourly contracts, as opposed to fixed price, would be easier to gauge if you can keep a client for at least 3 months. However, fixed-price contracts could be quite lengthy (i.e. large website build outs), so it is unclear how Upwork considers these types of contracts in their long-term client percentage statistics.

Recent account holds

The *My Stats* page provides statistics on recent account holds (within the past 90 days). Account holds are triggered by violating Upwork's terms of service. While the most common violation is receiving payment for work performed outside the Upwork platform, there are other violations capable of triggering a hold. These include account sharing, questionable identity, failure to perform on contracts, misrepresenting your business, your skills, your qualifications, or your services.

Also, contact information sharing, particularly in your profile, which must not include your phone, email, or other direct contact information, such as a Skype ID.

Excessive messaging, or spamming prospects with proposal and cover letter templates unrelated to the specifics of the job and/or the client's needs, can earn you an account hold. So can feedback abuse, which comprises pressuring clients to provide positive feedback by withholding work, or using other unethical ploys.

Account holds for any of the above reasons are reflected on your *My Stats* page and will strip you of your *Top Rated*, *Top Rated Plus*, or *Rising Talent* badge for 90 days *after* the resumption of your account. I cannot overstate the importance of abiding by Upwork's terms of service, as it is not a simple process to rectify account holds.

Reply rate

Also found in the *My Stats* section is reply rate, which is not based upon how often you reply to invitations, you should always reply, but on how quickly you reply. Installing the Upwork mobile app and allowing desktop notifications will enhance your ability to reply. Stay on the right side of this statistic by replying within 24 hours because this affects your Upwork ranking.

For one month, I reduced my reply rate from 100 percent to 50 percent and saw a 16 percent decrease in my invitations to interview. That means 16 percent fewer people invited me to jobs. As someone who gets 100+ job invites per month, that was a significant enough reduction from normal variations to know that the reply rate has an impact.

Marketing Effectiveness (*My Stats* Page)

Application frequency

By application frequency, Upwork means how many times you submitted job proposals in the prior 90 days

Application views

This is an important statistic that sheds light on the quality of your proposal. It compares your result to peers competing in the same category.

Interview rate

Again, a peer-to-peer comparison of the frequency your proposal results in an interview.

Hire rate

A peer-to-peer comparison of how often your interview results in your being hired.

Profile views

This statistic tells you how many times prospects discovered your profile in the past week and also provides a percentage change from the prior week's result. It speaks to the quality of your profile, especially in terms of keywords. Therefore, you must use keywords to structure your profile in such a way that it appears in client searches.

Click-through rate

No stats are directly available to you on click-through rates, although the four previous bullet points offer clues. While views are important, how often prospects click on your profile is more important. A quality picture and keyword rich headline are essential elements.

Understanding what prospects see in their search results will help you develop the best possible profile. Prospects see your picture, your headline, your JSS, your location, your hourly rate, and the number of hours you have worked, so clearly, these are the elements on which you must concentrate.

Feedback

So many aspects of your JSS hinge upon positive client feedback that I cannot stress too strongly its importance. Five star reviews coupled with glowing comments are crucial to your success as a freelancer. I often refer to it as the *lifeblood* of a successful freelancing career. Positive feedback is so important that I would encourage you to refund your client if you expect an unfavorable review is forthcoming. Refunded clients cannot submit a review.

Keywords

I touched on this earlier. It is important that you use a few keywords and keyword phrases throughout your profile, but particularly in your title and in the first paragraph of text.

Follow Upwork on social media where they publish an annual list of popular keywords searches used by clients. Use that list to choose keywords relevant to your line of work to increase your visibility and click-through rates.

Job success score (JSS)

In simple terms, your JSS represents your overall reputation by measuring the ratio of positive contract outcomes to negative contract outcomes.

Skills (tags)

Although my testing does not reveal that skill tags have a significant impact on ratings, they represent the services you can perform. Upwork allows a maximum of ten and I urge you to use all of them.

Categories

While categories do not impact your rankings, prospects use categories as a component in filtering freelancers for jobs, so make sure that yours reflect what you do.

Hourly rate

Your hourly rate appears prominently in client searches, appearing just below your profile photo. Consequently, it plays a significant role. Although your hourly rate, high or low, has no effect on your ranking, it impacts your click-through rate, which is a very important metric. Also worth noting, is the fact that clients can filter their freelancer searches by hourly rate.

Account activity

Upwork and clients want active freelancers. Log into Upwork a minimum of once every two weeks, and I need to stress—that is a minimum. Clients can filter by activity, and it is one of my favorite filters when searching for a freelancer to hire because active freelancers get back to me more quickly.

Freelancer type

Being a freelancer or an agency has no effect on your ranking, but there is a client filter for this category, so make certain that if you are listed in the agency category, that you can take on larger clients with very specific needs.

Location

Yes, clients can filter by location, but location does not affect your ranking. There is no point in using a false location. Upwork has safeguards in place to catch this unethical activity, so all you will accomplish by trying is being banned from the Upwork platform. It is common for people outside the U.S. who could fetch a higher rate by appearing to be in the U.S. to try to falsify their location. Upwork has seen this trick many times and isn't fooled, it's not worth the risk.

English proficiency level

Although this doesn't affect your ranking, clients can filter for this.

Experience level

Upwork will ask you to describe your experience level as entry level, intermediate or expert. Although this is an arbitrary answer, an honest answer will serve you well. You will only alienate clients by misrepresenting your abilities. You are setting yourself up for a bad review. Clients can filter for experience level, and clients have every right to expect candid evaluations.

Hours billed

The algorithm favors freelancers with higher numbers of hours worked, and they rank higher in search results. Clients can filter for hours worked before and after they post the job.

Jobs completed

Successfully completed jobs improve your ranking. Increasing your ranking through completed jobs will take time for those new to the platform. If you have clients that set multiple milestones, persuade them to set the milestones up as new jobs instead. You can improve your ranking more quickly this way. It is better for your profile to reflect three successfully completed jobs than one successfully completed job with three milestones. Use this tactic sparingly though, as it is easier on your client to just do milestones.

Profile visibility

Your profile's visibility is set to visible by default. You can go to *Profile Settings* and choose one of three visibility options, Public, Private, or Upwork users only. Obviously, you garner the most exposure from the Public setting.

Communication

Timely communications are important, and where these communications relate to invitations, they can affect your stats. I've already explained that excessive messaging can earn you an account hold, which will cost you any badge you may be holding.

Stay away from troubles by responding quickly and succinctly to your client. Upwork is not a social media platform—don't treat it like one. It is best to take your cues from the client. By all means, reach out if you have questions relative to the job at hand, but don't be a pest! For example, it is better to group five questions in one message than to send five different messages with one question each.

ALL ABOUT BADGES

Badges play a vital role in any successful freelancer's Upwork career. They represent a vote of confidence from Upwork's community of clients, which you can use to leverage your ability to get work on the platform.

Let me walk you through each of the four Upwork badges.

RISING TALENT

Upwork reserves the *Rising Talent* badge for its newest freelancers—those lacking a full *Work History* or *Job Success Score*.

Rising Talent badges are earned/awarded to 1) freelancers having a 100 percent complete profile that exhibits the freelancer's extensive experience outside the Upwork platform, 2) evidence of positive performance, such as high-quality proposals and success in being selected for jobs, and 3) full compliance with Upwork's *Terms of Service* (*TOS*).

Benefits

- The badge is prominently displayed in your profile.
- Fees on *Featured Jobs* are reduced to 10 percent.
- Recipients of the *Rising Talent* badge receive a one time bonus of 30 *Connects,*
- And they have access to a specialized customer support team via chat and ticket support.

Once the freelancer achieves an adequate *Work History*, the *Rising Talent* badge is automatically replaced by the JSS.

◈ TOP RATED

Top Rated badges are earned by freelancers (and agencies) who 1) show their ability to deliver high-quality work to multiple clients, 2) maintain a JSS of 90 percent or greater, 3) maintain an up-to-date, 100 percent complete profile, 4) accurately represent their availability for work, 5) have a strong earnings record, and 6) comply with Upwork's *TOS*.

Benefits

- A *Top Rated* badge displayed in your profile to all clients.
- Reduced fees (beginning at 10 percent) on *Featured Jobs*. These *Featured Job* clients have paid Upwork an additional fee to have their post standout from the crowd. Apart from the *Featured Job* banner and reduced fees for freelancers, these jobs are no different from any other job posted on Upwork.
- The privilege of making occasional requests to remove client feedback.
- Automatic enrollment to the *Jobs Digest* email, which matches your skills to open jobs on the Upwork platform and notifies you to apply.
- Upwork waives the 5-day security hold for Top Rated freelancers and agencies so you are paid five days earlier than freelancers and agencies not holding the *Top Rated* badge.
- Eligible for *Premium* customer support by phone or chat.
- Upwork's *Talent Specialists* working on behalf of clients, may single you out for job invitations based upon your skills. This is a free service that increases your visibility to clients, You need not enroll, as the service kicks in upon receipt of your *Top Rated* badge. Jobs secured by invitation are *Connect* free!
- You have the option to opt out of this program.

TOP RATED PLUS

To earn the *Top Rated Plus* badge freelancers (and agencies) must have a successful track record with long-term and/or large contracts. These freelancers (and agencies) receive repeated positive feedback on all their contracts, including high-value contracts. These freelancers represent Upwork's top three percent.

Top Rate Plus badges are earned by freelancers (and agencies) that 1) have $10,000 ($20,000 for agencies) in total earnings over the previous 12 months while maintaining their *Top Rated* status, and 2) have worked on at least one large contract (ten percent of all contracts for agencies) in the prior 12 months with no negative outcomes.

Note: Individual freelancers can only qualify for Top Rated Plus by being a Non-Exclusive Agency Contractor.

Benefits

- Prominent display of the *Top Rated Plus* badge in the freelancer's profile.
- Reduced fees for featured jobs (starting with a ten percent reduction).
- Able to request feedback removal.
- Invitations assisted by Upwork's *Talent Specialists*.
- Automatic enrollment in the *Jobs Digest* program.
- Waiver of the 5-day security hold for hourly contracts.
- Premium customer support.

EXPERT-VETTED

Expert-Vetted is a badge reserved for Upwork's top one percent. Only freelancers in Web, Mobile and Software Development; Design and Creative; and Sales and Marketing are eligible for this badge. These freelancers (and agencies) have been tested by Upwork's technical *Talent Managers* for their expertise and soft skills to ensure they are of the highest quality, professional, and have excellent communication skills. Freelancers do not start this process—it is by invitation only!

Benefits

- The *Expert-Vetted* badge on a freelancer's profile establishes them as the best-of-the-best.

- *Expert-Vetted* badge holders enjoy all the privileges of *Top Rated Plus* badge holders.

- Upwork says additional benefits are on the way! I'll keep you posted.

ALL ABOUT THE JOB SUCCESS SCORE (JSS)

If you take away nothing else from this section/chapter, take away this: Be obsessed with your *Job Success Score*. I say this because so much hinges on your JSS. Your badges for one. You cannot receive a *Top Rated*, *Top Rated Plus*, or *Expert-Vetted* badge with a JSS of less than 90 percent. Badges are important, which makes your JSS equally important. While newcomers to the Upwork platform may be awarded the *Rising Talent* badge, the moment that their *Work History* becomes sufficient, Upwork replaces the *Rising Talent* badge with your JSS, whether the JSS is good or bad.

This begs the question, how is my Job Success Score calculated, what are the components, and what level of control do I have over my JSS?

In the simplest of explanations, Upwork determines your JSS by subtracting your negative outcomes (feedback), N in the equation, from your positive (successful) outcomes, P in the equation, and dividing the result by total outcomes (P-N÷Total = JSS). Upwork calculates JSS scores in rolling windows of 6, 12, and 24 month intervals, and the highest of these scores becomes your JSS. You may encounter differing reports from unscrupulous pretenders, but I assure you that Upwork uses the highest score, not the lowest, and not an average. I have verified this with Upwork's management.

Unfortunately, the overall JSS is more complex than this simple formula implies. Feedback is just one element of the JSS, which also includes long-term relationships, inactive contracts, and private feedback. You'll be happy to know that as of November 2020, Upwork discontinued its practice of counting contracts that end with no feedback as negative outcomes in the JSS calculation.

At least three additional factors impact the JSS. They are:

Inactive contracts

You should carefully monitor hourly and fixed price jobs listed as *In Progress* in your profile's *Work History*. If they languish for too long with no activity, they have the potential to lower your JSS. If you have dormant jobs *In Progress,* it's a good idea to reach out to those clients and request they end the contract and provide feedback.

Long-term relationships

Upwork's JSS calculations smile favorably on long-term relationships. These relationships may take the form of active *In Progress* jobs and also repeat business from previous clients over a long time period. To be more specific, the percentage of clients that continue to give you work for at least three months.

Private Feedback

Most freelancers are keenly aware of the impact public feedback has on their JSS, however, few are aware of the significant impact private feedback has on their score. Private feedback is requested of every client when a contract ends.

Upwork assures clients that this feedback will never be shared, and it never is. Clients are asked to rate freelancers on a scale of one to ten, with ten being the best possible rating. This feedback is, by design, different from the public 5-star feedback with which we are all familiar. I say, by design, because Upwork understands many clients promise a 5-star rating in their job post, while other clients are simply reluctant to post a negative review. The private feedback Upwork receives from clients allows them to form a realistic picture of freelancer performance.

Don't worry too much about difficult clients that have left negative feedback, public or private. Upwork's algorithm detects patterns of unreasonable client behavior and feedback from these clients will not count against you.

One final factor that impacts a freelancer's JSS is the frequency of hires. The *Marketing effectiveness* section of the *My Stats* page will provide clues on this subject. In the example below, you see this freelancer has only applied to 12 jobs in the past 90 days. This is not a high level of activity, averaging about one proposal per week. The algorithm likes activity.

You were viewed stats speak to the effectiveness of the freelancer's profile, specifically regarding keywords and the impact of the title and first paragraph of the overview.

You were interviewed results address the quality of the freelancer's proposal.

You were hired data suggests the freelancer interviews well and makes a persuasive pitch.

Your profile was discovered tells the freelancer how often their profile received clicks during the week.

Marketing effectiveness

You've applied to **12 jobs** in the past 90 days. Compared to your peers:

Among freelancers in Writing

	Less often	More often
You were viewed		
You were interviewed		
You were hired		

Your profile was discovered **1 time** last week. (**-50%** from the previous week)

Use these statistics as a guide to improve relative aspects of your profile. Activity, clicks, interviews, and hires all impact the algorithm and by extension, your JSS. Don't be afraid to experiment!

RECOVERING FROM A BAD JSS

When your JSS tumbles, it seems like a career-ending catastrophe. The good news—it isn't! Recovering from a JSS that has plummeted, however, requires some serious effort.

The first step is to determine the cause. If you don't understand why your JSS took a hit, it will happen again. I've listed the eight most common causes below.

Negative *Public Feedback* on a significant percentage of small jobs.

Think of small (low value) contracts as battles and a positive JSS (90 percent +) as the war. This helps put the impact of *Public Feedback* for low-value contracts in perspective. You can lose a few battles and still win the war, but lose too many battles and you lose the war. Always keep the basic formula for the JSS top of mind—subtract negative outcomes (feedback) from positive (successful) outcomes and divide the result by total outcomes. Just to remind you, this is the formula where P equals the number of positive outcomes and N equals the number of negative outcomes (P-N÷Total = JSS).

How to recover?

Remember the formula! It is basically a percentage, which you can improve by landing and completing jobs that end with positive feedback. In other words, increase the value of *P* in the above equation.

Negative *Public Feedback* on a large contract (high value job).

How to recover?

In this scenario, you can achieve a recovery in much the same way as outlined above, increasing the value of P. This isn't easy, because high-value contracts carry more weight than low-value contracts and you will need many small jobs with positive feedback to overcome a single incidence of negative *Public Feedback*. Alternatively, land high-value jobs, do outstanding work, don't over-promise and under-deliver, and earn 5-star *Public Feedback*.

Upwork provides the freelancer with the ability to allow clients to change their feedback. To get to this screen, click My Jobs in the menu bar, then select *Contracts* from the drop-down menu. Then scroll to the job that you want to offer the client the opportunity to change feedback and click on the job title. At the top of the screen you will see this ribbon.

MILESTONES & EARNINGS   MESSAGES & FILES   TERMS & SETTINGS   FEEDBACK ●

Selecting FEEDBACK will bring you to the screen below, and then just click on *Enable client to change feedback*.

Client's Feedback to You

No Feedback Received
Enable client to change feedback

Try communicating with the client. If the poor rating was undeserved, make the case, and encourage the client to improve your rating.

If you are unsuccessful in getting the client to change your rating, then you must make your case by responding to the client's rating. While this will not improve your score, it may increase your ability to land future jobs. Be factual and respectful.

Negative *Private Feedback*.

How to recover?

Whether you have received negative *Private Feedback* is largely unknowable—it's private! There is a clue, however, and we addressed that earlier in the chapter on *Understanding the Algorithm*. If you will recall, this clue appears on the *My Stats* page (see below). If you see a significant drop in the percentage of *Clients who would recommend you*, then chances are you have been the victim of negative *Private Feedback*.

Client satisfaction

Job Success score	12-month earnings	$3,678.09
96% Job Success		
	Clients who would recommend you	90%
My Badges		
TOP RATED	Long-term clients	27%
Last updated Jan 24	Recent account holds	0
	Top Rated eligible weeks	16 of 16

Even if you are reasonably certain which one of your clients gave you negative *Private Feedback* and convinced them to change it, Upwork's policies make no provision for the client to do so.

Top Rated and Top Rated Plus freelancers may exercise their occasional right to remove feedback. However, this only applies to *Public Feedback*. *Private Feedback* cannot be removed, therefore your JSS may not change, and may even fall further if you delete positive *Public Feedback* in a futile attempt to delete *Private Feedback*. Only you can weigh the risk vs. benefit of taking this action.

Dormant (inactive) jobs in your *Work History*.

How to Recover?

If you follow Upwork's forum, this subject has been hotly debated. The consensus, however, is that inactive jobs pose no threat to your JSS unless there has been zero monetary activity. As long as money has changed hands between client and freelancer, further inactivity does not count against your JSS, so make certain that happens!

Past positive feedback drops from the calculation because the moving window has placed them outside the scoring formula's time-frame.

How to recover?

The preferred method for avoiding the perils of the moving window is to maintain a consistent record of high-quality work that earns 5-star *Public Feedback*. As I've explained, Upwork calculates JSS scores in rolling windows of 6, 12, and 24 month intervals, and the highest of these scores becomes your JSS.

So if, for example, the initial 6 months of your Upwork career was outstanding, and earned you a positive JSS, but over the following 6 months you turned in a lackluster performance. This diminishes your JSS in the 12-month window because you have increased the denominator in the equation (P-N÷Total = JSS). As time passes, and the initial 6-month window falls out of the JSS calculation, your JSS will decline, all else being equal. It's worth repeating. A *consistent* record of high-quality work that earns 5-star *Public Feedback* is key to a positive JSS.

Poor *Marketing Effectiveness*

Marketing effectiveness has three components, 1) views, 2) interviews, and 3) hires.

Marketing effectiveness

You've applied to **11 jobs** in the past 90 days. Compared to your peers:

	Among freelancers in Writing	
You were viewed ◄	Less often	More often
You were interviewed ◄	Less often	More often
You were hired ◄	Less often	More often

How to recover?

Extended periods of inactivity can hurt your JSS. As I've said before, the Upwork algorithm loves activity. The real problem rests with invitations. If you're going to be away from the platform for any reason, vacation, hospital stay, whatever—set your profile to *Not Available*. By doing this, you protect your JSS from being dinged for slow response times to invitations.

Loss of *Long-term Relationships*

Long-term relationships are calculated on a percentage basis. This percentage is found on the *My Stats* page under *Client satisfaction*, which shows where you stand in terms of long-term contracts. It is generally accepted that 25 percent and above improves your JSS. Conversely, if you lose enough long-term relationships to cause your percentage to dip below twenty-five, the impact on your JSS will be negative.

Job Success score	12-month earnings	$3,678.09
96% Job Success		
	Clients who would recommend you	90%
My Badges		
TOP RATED	Long-term clients	27%
Last updated Feb 7		
	Recent account holds	0

How to recover?

Your best option for developing long-term relationships is found through hourly jobs, which provide increased opportunities for long-term interaction with your clients.

Hiring frequency drops dramatically

Accepting and/or winning fewer jobs can negatively impact your JSS. Upwork uses only accepted contracts as the basis for determining your JSS.

How to recover?

It is important to understand that when you have fewer jobs, negative feedback will have a greater effect on your score. For example, one incidence of negative feedback out of five will carry more weight than 2 instances out of twenty.

Clearly, the best course of action is to apply for more jobs, draft winning proposals, and accept more contracts. I will expand on drafting winning proposals later, in the chapter titled *How to Create High Converting Proposals that Will Wow Your Prospects*.

TOP 12 THINGS YOU SHOULD NEVER DO ON UPWORK

All businesses have policies, and Upwork is no exception. Upwork designs its policies to protect the business and its clients. Respect, follow, and understand these policies. Online businesses refer to these policies as Terms of Service (TOS).

Upwork's TOS, like all others, is a dull read, but I recommend you do so anyway. I'll be covering some of the most common violations in this chapter, but please don't assume it is comprehensive. What follows is best described as a list of dos and don'ts.

Do not violate *any* of Upwork's policies! Once your account is banned, it is nearly impossible to get it reinstated. These are the most common violations:

1.] Do not provide contact information in your profile or proposal. You may not share contact information until a contract is agreed upon and accepted by both the prospect and freelancer. Contact information includes email addresses, Skype IDs, phone numbers, or any other direct contact information.

2.] Do not agree to any payment arrangements with a prospect outside of the Upwork platform. Clients *and* freelancers pay fees to Upwork. This provides an incentive for clients *and* freelancers to arrange for payment outside of Upwork's platform. It's not worth getting caught!

3.] Do not impersonate anyone else. Do not use someone else's photo for your profile. Do not falsify your location. It's not worth it.

4.] Do not allow anyone else to use your Upwork account. For example, your friend's account has been placed on hold for a TOS violation and the friend asks your permission to use your account. The answer must always be NO!

5.] Do not engage in spam or harassment. You must treat everyone on Upwork with the utmost respect and courtesy. I have used many platforms that provide leads to freelancers and Upwork stands out as the platform where freelancers are responsive, honest, professional, and courteous. Aggressive statements, insults, and repeated follow up attempts to prospects who don't respond is not a business practice you want to engage in.

6.] Do not bribe clients for positive feedback. Great feedback is earned, not extorted. While it is perfectly alright to make sure that clients understand the importance of positive feedback (public and private) to the success of any freelancer, never cross the line by saying or offering something that may be construed as coercion or bribery.

7.] Do not fail to perform on your contract with your client. Much like writing a check is a promise to pay, accepting a contract is the equivalent of a promise to complete the job to the best of your ability.

8.] Do not misrepresent or exaggerate your qualifications, services, or skills. To do so will only bring grief to you and to your client. Grief to you in the form of a negative *Public* and/or *Private Feedback*, and grief to your client resulting from your poor work product. It is even possible that a payment dispute will arise.

One through eight above are TOS violations. TOS violations can trigger a minimum 90-day account hold, which, incidentally, strips you of any badge you may have earned. To quote Upwork, "Account holds lead to account interruptions, and consequences could include the inability to continue working on Upwork and the loss of your hard-earned reputation."

Items nine through twelve below are *not* TOS violations but they are things you should not do if you want a successful freelancing experience on Upwork.

1.] Do not ignore job invitations. Even when the job invitation comes at a bad time, does not align with your skills, or just does not suit you...respond! This is not only the polite way to handle an invitation, but failing to respond can give prospects a negative impression. Remember, prospects can see your response time, and you don't want them to see that it is greater than 24 hours. Be courteous—respond, even if you are declining the offer. It takes only seconds to decline.

2.] Do not let your profile become stale. Rotate keywords regularly and test the effects of any changes you make in what should be an ongoing effort to improve your profile. Make only one change at a time. Leave the change in place for at least one month and watch the *My Stats* page for any changes, positive or negative, concentrating on the *Marketing effectiveness* section of *My Stats*.

3.] Do not accept jobs unless you research the client. Remember, every contract represents a risk for negative *Public* or *Private Feedback*. Review *Avoid Catastrophe: Researching Your Prospect Is the First Crucial Step* in the *Convert* section of this book.

4.] Do not make it a chore for prospects to respond to your proposals. Instead, try to start a dialogue by asking easy to respond to pertinent questions.

SECTION 3

CONVERT

AVOID CATASTROPHE: RESEARCHING YOUR PROSPECT IS THE FIRST CRUCIAL STEP

As freelancers, we often feel that we're under the microscope—*Private Feedback, Public Feedback, Job Success Scores*—it can be quite stressful. Clients receive a *Public Feedback* score too, but as freelancers, we need to understand that these are not always meaningful because many freelancers are fearful of giving a client a bad score. Why bite the hand that feeds you?

This chapter will not only help you mitigate the risk of negative *Public* and *Private Feedback,* but also prevent you from wasting *Connects.* After all, one negative review can crash your JSS and *Connects,* for the most part, aren't free.

You should conduct your research on the prospect before you submit a proposal. Although it is possible to withdraw the proposal, you have spent your *Connects* and Upwork will not refund them just because you changed your mind.

Your approach to researching a prospect must be methodical. Don't worry, after you develop a system, it becomes almost second nature and, once you know what to look for, it only takes a couple of minutes. It is important to accomplish your research quickly because you want to be among the first to submit your proposal. While prospects don't necessarily receive proposals in the order submitted ("best result" matches may rise to the top), the prospect's screen still shows just ten proposals per page, so if you are number 35, it is unlikely that the prospect will make it to your proposal. Therefore, prospect research begins with a strategically designed job filter.

Configuring the Filter

Begin by selecting the *Category* that best aligns with your chosen niche. Click on *Select Categories* to reveal the list and make your choice(s). The filter allows you to check multiple boxes. Then choose the *Experience Level* or levels you wish to include in your search. The number in parentheses represents the number of jobs available in each selection. This is followed by *Job Type* where you can choose hourly, fixed price, or both.

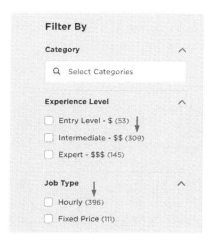

I will not insult your intelligence by walking you through every available filter. Instead, let's focus on filters that have the potential to eliminate undesirable jobs. The first on the list is the Number of Proposals filter shown below. Logically, if a job post has already received 20 or more proposals. The chance of a prospect seeing your proposal is not good! I would recommend checking only the first two or three boxes.

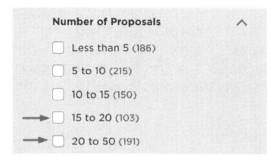

Second, is *Client Info*. This filter tells you at a glance if any of your previous clients have posted a job. Upwork also provides this information through the *Notifications* page. If you have had a positive experience with your former client and the job fits your skill set, it's a good idea to reach out. This helps you build relationships. If *My Previous Clients* is at zero, then you must consider checking *Payment Verified*. While prospects with a *Payment Verified* status may give you that warm, fuzzy feeling, consider that you might eliminate some worthy clients whose only sin is not having taken the time to set up their payment method.

Third is *Client History*. This filter gives you the option to explore the jobs offered by prospects with no experience, intermediate experience, or substantial experience. Personally, I do not believe there are right or wrong choices in this category. Prospects with no hires may need hand-holding, whereas prospects with 10+ hires are likely well-versed on the platform.

Last is *Client Location*. Freelancers have varying comfort levels. Some may prefer to work with prospects in their own country. Others may prefer to work with native English speaking prospects. The *Client Location* category can be of help to such freelancers. There is no right or wrong selection—personal preference should be your guide.

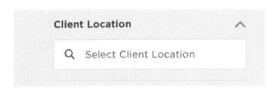

These handy filters help with preliminary prospect research, but they only take the process so far. When you select a job that interests you and click on the posting, the opportunity for additional research begins.

What stands out in the posting below?

1.] It is unusual to see so few proposals on a 4-day-old job posting.

2.] An almost 5-star review—no surprise there!

3.] The average hourly rate is rather low.

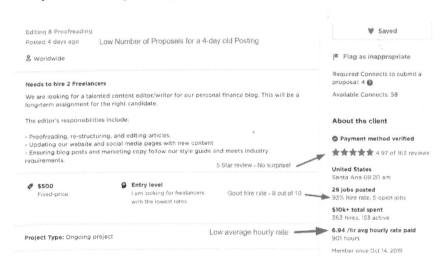

Digging deeper, we see that the prospect has:

1.] Already hired 2 freelancers (fulfilling his stated quota.)
2.] Sent 15 invitations of which 10 have gone unanswered.

Preferred qualifications

English level: ❷ Native or Bilingual ✅

Activity on this job

Proposals: ❷ 10 to 15

Last viewed by client: ❷ 3 days ago

Hires: 2 ◄

Interviewing: 2

Invites sent: 15

Unanswered invites: 10

Looking through the *Client's recent history*, I see several red flags. The first, a 2.4-star review. Second, the absence of feedback from the client.

Share Your Opinion About Financial Products | Dec 2020 - Dec 2020
★★⯨☆☆ I don't know why but I just got 7 cent from this | Fixed-price $22.00
To freelancer: Keira N.No feedback given

Share Your Opinion About Financial Products | Dec 2020 - Dec 2020
★★★★★ I enjoyed working with client, requirements were easily explained and expectations were laid out | Fixed-price $22.00
accordingly. Client responded quickly when communication was initiated. I enjoyed working with the client and
would recommend them in the future. less
To freelancer: Leigha W.No feedback given ▲

Below are several more from the *Client's recent history* where no feedback was given on either side.

Share Your Opinion About Financial Products | Jan 2021 - Feb 2021
No feedback given | Fixed-price $22.00
To freelancer: David B.No feedback given

Share Your Opinion About Financial Products | Oct 2020 - Feb 2021
No feedback given | Fixed-price $20.00
To freelancer: Jumoke A.No feedback given

Share Your Opinion About Financial Products | Oct 2020 - Feb 2021
No feedback given | Fixed-price $22.00
To freelancer: Samuel A.No feedback given

Share Your Opinion About Financial Products | Dec 2020 - Feb 2021
No feedback given | Fixed-price $20.00
To freelancer: Edwin M.No feedback given

Share Your Opinion About Financial Products | Dec 2020 - Feb 2021
No feedback given | Fixed-price $22.00
To freelancer: Yusuf E.No feedback given

Let's summarize what we have learned from our research.

- No one is beating down the door to work for this prospect. The job posting is 4 days old and we see only 10 to 15 proposals. This prospect has sent out 15 invitations and received only 5 responses.

- Although, to be fair, the prospect acknowledges they are looking for the cheapest rate, the prospect's average hourly rate is quite low.

- Two freelancers have been hired for this job, meeting the prospect's stated requirement. If you submit a proposal in these circumstances, you may be wasting your *Connects*.

- The prospect received a 2.4-star review, which is very unsettling. Freelancers are usually reluctant to offer negative feedback to clients.

- The prospect doesn't leave feedback for their freelancers, and while this doesn't hurt your JSS, it does not help it either.

- The prospect's history shows no instances of repeat hires, which may suggest that the prospect is very hard to please, or it may suggest that freelancers have no interest in working for this prospect again.

Contrast that with the *Client review history* below. This prospect takes the time to enter a review *and* comment on the freelancer's performance. Unlike the former prospect, their history shows repeat hiring, which speaks to the sincerity of the review. You will frequently see prospects that say "will definitely hire again!" but the *Client review history* doesn't reflect any occurrences of rehiring past freelancers.

Article Writer needed

Jan 2021 - Jan 2021
Fixed-price $20.01

★★★★★Working with Justice is always a pleasure. He knows what he wants, which makes it easier for the task to be completed satisfactorily.

To freelancer: Akinwunmi A. ★★★★★Having worked with over five different freelance writers over the years, I can honestly say that Akinwunmi is one of the best writers I have worked with. Not only did he meet the deadline, his communication skills are top-notch. He understood our needs and expectations and provided excellent work. He has now become our first point of contact for all future projects. less

One page Business plan needed

Jan 2021 - Jan 2021
Fixed-price $20.00

No feedback given

To freelancer: Victory E. ★★★★★Victory was proficient in her writing. I was impressed.

Quick Research Description:

Jan 2021 - Jan 2021
Fixed-price $5.00

★★★★★Highly recommended

To freelancer: Oshomoji O. ★★★★★Professional freelancer. Highly recommended.

Article Writer needed

Jan 2021 - Jan 2021
Fixed-price $20.00

★★★★★He was easy to work with and started his requirements clearly.

To freelancer: Akinwunmi A. ★★★★★"Akinwunmi was a pleasure to work with. He is efficient, hardworking, and he managed to get the job done in a timely and efficient manner. Would definitely recommend him and rehire him in the future." less

You need to understand that these interpretations and conclusions are subjective, however, you must read between the lines to avoid exposing yourself to difficult clients that burn up *Connects* and do nothing to advance your JSS.

HOW TO CREATE HIGH CONVERTING PROPOSALS THAT WILL WOW YOUR PROSPECTS

Let's begin by defining what a proposal is so that we are all on the same page. A proposal is the initial query into a job opportunity. For our purposes, *proposal* and *bid* carry the same meaning and are interchangeable terms.

Prospects are busier, have more choices, and higher expectations than ever before. Couple these facts with an exploding number of freelancers and you will understand why a powerful, standout, succinct proposal is so important.

Submitting a proposal begins with the click of the *Submit a Proposal* button in the upper right-hand corner of the job posting (top arrow). To the right of the bottom arrow is the button that activates Upwork's *Save Job* feature. While the *Save Job* feature can be useful for some, for others, it becomes a crutch for the procrastinator that lurks within us all. Too often, saved jobs aren't viewed again until they are well past their expiry date! Use this feature sparingly.

If you are using my *aggregated listening technique* and have set up your RSS feed, you will learn that you have no practical use for the *Save Job* feature.

I've made it clear throughout the book that I have done years of testing to determine what works best on Upwork's platform and proposals are no exception. Testing has shown that proposals of over 100 words convert at a 24.3 percent rate, while proposals with less than 100 words convert at a rate of 27 percent. In other words, keeping your proposal under 100 words increases your response rate by 11.1 percent—that's huge! In a separate test, I found that including a video link in the proposal raised my response rate from 25.9 percent to 31 percent, which is an increase of almost 20 percent. When you consistently combine these two key elements in your proposals, it could mean thousands more dollars in revenue through increased client acquisition—that's really huge!

Before you submit your proposal, ask yourself if it accomplishes the following objectives:

- Does it make me stand out?
- Have I shown the prospect who I am and that I am a good fit?
- Did I show the prospect that my skill set and/or experiences are relevant to the job?
- Have I motivated the prospect to respond?

Components of a Great Proposal

1.] Always create customized text that is specifically tailored to the prospect's project. Cookie-cutter language and cut & paste proposals are unacceptable to most prospects and your proposal will be dismissed out-of-hand. You must reference the prospect's project and show that you understand what they need done. This gives your proposal credibility with the prospect.

Your proposal will get a 3.8 percent better response rate (I know because I've tested this) if you reference the prospect by name. I know—rarely does a job posting include the name of the client. However, I'll share this trick that will reveal the prospect's name in most instances. The greater the amount the prospect has spent on Upwork, the more likely it is that you will learn their name. Here is an example from a job posting. Note that the client has spent $5,000+ on hiring freelancers for previous Upwork projects.

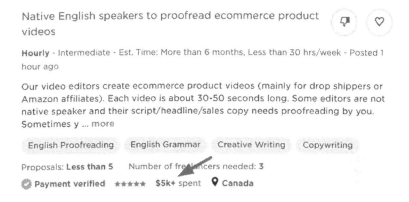

Scrolling through the prospect's reviews, you can quickly find an example of a freelancer that has referred to the client by name.

I like to find a second example, just to erase any doubt about the accuracy of the name, and as you see below, another freelancer has confirmed the prospect's name to be *Roger*.

Upload course contents from D2L (Brightspace) to Moodle   Dec 2020 · Dec 2020
★★★★★ Roger is the most wonderful boss any freelancer would ask for. He is very understanding,   165 hrs @ $3.00/hr
patient, responsive and gives a reasonable deadline and worki ... more   Billed: $493.50
To freelancer: Gayle anne D. ★★★★★ You can't go wrong if you decide to hire Gayle. I am extremely impressed with her quality of work and positive attitude. It's very pleasant to work wi ... more

2.] Tell the prospect who you are and refer to past jobs and former clients that you have helped in similar circumstances. This instills trust in the prospect.

3.] Appeal to the prospect's needs and *pain points*. Pain points are specific problems that your prospect is experiencing. Pain points are problems, plain and simple. Let the prospect know that you have the experience required to solve these problems, and you enjoy doing the type of work needed to resolve them. This shows the prospect that you have done it before and can do it again, which also builds trust.

4.] Create a custom video. Use Loom.com or similar services to create a short video to include in your proposal via hyperlink. Do you want a leg-up on your competition? As I've mentioned before, I am not only an Upwork freelancer; I am also an employer, and I can tell you from personal experience that 98 percent of the proposals I receive do not include a video. Remember, a custom video boosts your response rate by 20 percent!

5.] Keep your proposal short, on point, and polite. Convey confidence—not arrogance.

I want to share these helpful tools—tools that will enhance your proposal response time, increase prospect response rates, and improve your overall productivity. They are:

Auto Text Expander

Auto Text Expander is a free Google Chrome Extension. Just type *Free Auto Text Expander for Google Chrome* into your browser and click on it. That brings up the screen you see below. Then click on the Add to Chrome button.

That brings you to this screen, where you can program your shortcuts. Adding a shortcut is easy. Click on *Add* (top arrow) and insert the shortcut (bottom arrow) followed by the text that you want to insert whenever you type the shortcut. Each time you add a shortcut, remember to click on *Refresh* and *Save*. This activates the shortcuts you have entered. I urge you to test your shortcuts. If you see that you've made an error, trash it, and start over.

Loom.com

This free resource, Loom.com, will make creating custom videos for your proposal almost effortless. When you open Loom.com, you will see the following screen. The website is very user friendly, so there is no need to walk you through the details.

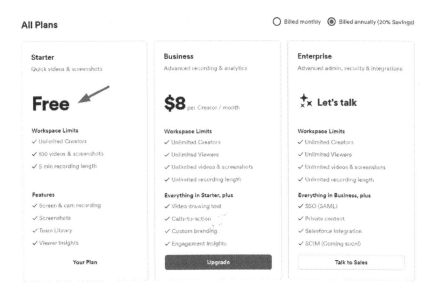

Sample High Converting Proposal Letter

I created the following sample for you to use as an inspirational guide. Make it your own, using the skyscraper technique you learned earlier in the book.

Hi [Insert Prospect's Name],

*Improve your response rate 4 percent by using the prospect's name. Use the **trick** I showed you earlier!*

Interesting job post. Too often, I just see "need help" in these posts, so the detail you provided was great.

Give the prospect a compliment—flattery will get you everywhere!

I'm a CMO and have built and sold 4 of my own companies. I have experience managing teams of experts with multi-million dollar budgets as well as creating marketing strategies for startups bringing their product/service to market.

Tell the prospect who you are. Talk about your skills and experiences, making certain that they align with the prospect's needs.

I made this video for you: loom.com/ sofhasodfi9823lidfoas8dfasd

This is the personal touch that has the added benefit of increasing your response rate by nearly 20 percent!

Do you need an entrepreneurial-minded marketing leader?

Ask an easy-to-answer leading question that addresses the prospect's pain point and also encourages a response from the prospect.

Let's schedule a quick discovery call. Please provide two dates and times that work for you this week.

*This is a **call to action** intended to elicit a response from the prospect and works in concert with your **leading question**, but you aren't **asking** the prospect to do this, you're **telling** him to do this.*

-Mike

P.S. Be sure to check out my profile. One of my 5-star reviews is from [Insert Name], where I completed a job very similar to yours.

Referring to your review encourages the prospect to look at your profile. This is especially important if you are applying for the job rather than responding to an invitation. Obviously, if you received an invitation, the prospect has looked at your profile. In terms of being read, email studies show postscripts are second only to subject lines.

Final Thoughts

If you stick to the guidelines I have outlined above, your proposal won't take a long time to create, but these few minutes will land you more jobs and more money. The principal objective of your proposal is to snag the interview, not to get hired on the spot. If you focus on getting hired, your proposal gets bogged down in details and the prospect may lose interest. After all, having interviewed, you may decide that you don't want the job!

HOW TO GET A FLOOD OF INVITES AND SCORE MORE CLIENTS

What is an Upwork Invitation? It is like being pre-selected to apply for a credit card. The card issuer has looked at your credit report, noted your credit score, your debt ratio, and other important factors, and concluded that you would be an excellent candidate for their credit card, so they invite you to apply. When you receive an Upwork invitation to interview, it means the prospect has clicked on your profile, noted your JSS, your *Public Feedback*, and other key factors, and concluded that you would be a fit candidate for the job.

You are notified of this invitation by email, and through the Notifications tab in Upwork.

Find Work   My Jobs   Reports   Messages   ?   🔔   ▷

Click on the bell and look for the rocket icon, which is associated with job invites and other critical notifications.

🚀   You have received an invitation to interview for the job
      January 6

Personally, I receive three to four invites per day. My testing shows that getting an invitation means you are 3 times more likely to win the job. Sadly, my research also shows that 82 percent of invitations go unanswered. This is unacceptable! Not only is it discourteous, but it also impacts the response time stats in the *Communication* section of your *My Stats* page.

While your failure to respond to invitations within 24 hours, or at all, is *not* considered by the Upwork algorithm, it *is* reflected in your profile (see below) and may deter prospects from extending future invitations. You don't want this! After all, when you apply to a job via invitation, it doesn't cost you any *Connects*! Freelancers that apply to invitations within one hour are practically a shoo-in for the job. If you *aren't* interested in the job, an invitation still deserves a polite decline within 24 hours. You may not be aware of this, but clients are only allowed a maximum of three free invitations per job posting, after which they must pay a fee.

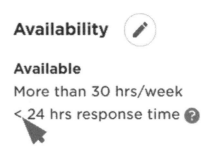

So, how do you generate more invitations? I've identified six key factors:

1.] Maintain a 100 percent complete profile.

2.] Ensure that your portfolio displays the most current examples of your work. Outdated portfolio items are off-putting and suggest to the prospect that perhaps your best days are behind you.

3.] Continuously experiment with your title and make sure it is compelling (clickable). Be attentive to the keywords you use in your title, making certain your keywords correspond to the work you do. Use them frequently in your introduction and always reference your highest and best work.

4.] Maintain a JSS of at least 90 percent, or, if you are a new freelancer, work on getting *Rising Star* status.

5.] Quality writing converts! Editing your own writing is a challenge, so consider hiring a freelance copywriter on Upwork to review your title and introduction. Use the following link to access recommended copywriters that can make your Upwork profile read flawlessly: https://freelancermasterclass.com/upworkmastery-book/

6.] Test—Test!!—and Test again!!! Rotate keywords in your title and in your introduction. For example, *Great Designer with 10 Years' Experience* could be changed to *Great WordPress Website Designer with 10 Years' Experience*. Experiment with a variety of profile photos using Photofeeler.com, and don't be afraid to experiment with your title.

Review your *My Stats* page frequently. The *My Stats* page reflects your results on the characteristics Upwork has defined as being crucial to your success. As these stats improve, so will the frequency of your invitations!

HOW TO SAVE YOUR BEST CLIENTS USING THE PML TECHNIQUE

Early in the book, we talked about the ups and downs freelancers will experience in their income. We also discussed the necessity of adding a ten percent cushion in our hourly rate to compensate for these inevitable difficulties.

This is no revelation, but we often lose sight of the fact that our clients' businesses also have ups and downs. Sometimes clients want to keep working with us, but because of a money crunch, they don't have the cash flow to keep freelancers on. In a money crunch, freelancers will get cut before full-time staff. That is why I developed my PML technique. This technique allows both parties to keep working. PML is an acronym for Pay Me Later.

Don't worry, I am not suggesting you work for free. However, I am asking you to put some faith in your client, much like they put faith in you when they hired you. In order to use the PML technique effectively, your client should meet the following criteria:

- A long and consistent history of working together. The length could be 3 months or 3 years, whatever you feel is comfortable to gauge what a solid working relationship would be.
- A history of consistent and timely payments.

- A business model you believe has a future.

- A staff you believe can grow the business.

- A genuine feeling that the business has upside in the near future.

Reserve this technique for long-term clients, clients who value your work, have shown their loyalty, and have paid you repeatedly, on time, without fail.

The benefits of the PML technique are:

- The client continues to receive the services needed.

- The freelancer remains on the job.

- It makes an already strong working relationship even stronger.

This is difficult to implement on Upwork's platform, but you can accomplish it on fixed price jobs through milestones. For example, if the total fixed price for the job is $1500, establish milestones with nominal payments ($25.00 for example) and create a final milestone that is essentially a balloon payment for the bulk of your work. This will keep your client's costs at a minimum. Work this out with your client based on mutually agreed terms.

If the job is hourly, ask your client to transition it to fixed price.

This is not a tool that you should use lightly. There is a risk of loss which you must weigh against the potential benefit. However, I have found it to be an effective technique and a wonderful client saver when used properly.

MAKING A KILLER VIDEO

The three most important reasons for including a video in your profile are: 1) a video will make your profile stand out, 2) a video helps you create an emotional connection with prospects, 3) a video will get you more responses.

I've mentioned this before, but it bears repeating. Only a fraction of freelance profiles includes a video, so a video automatically makes you stand out from the crowd. A video gives prospects the opportunity to connect with you, and to learn how your skill set can help resolve their problems.

This chapter will speak to the production elements that should be considered in creating your video, how to convey a persuasive message through your video that will deliver results, and a few technical tips that will enhance the impact of your video. First, the production elements.

Camera

Don't delay posting your video because you feel you don't have the right equipment. Do you have a smartphone? If you have a video capable smartphone, then you can create your profile video. Obviously, use the best camera available to you and if that's a smartphone—use it!

Lighting

Lighting can make or break your video. Avoid shadows and sitting in front of windows. Ring lights are inexpensive and produce excellent results. If you wear glasses, be aware of reflected glare. If you can manage without your glasses, do so.

Sound

Choose a quiet spot to record your video. Traffic noises, dogs barking, children playing, are distractions you should avoid. Your viewers must be able to focus on you and hear your message clearly.

Frankly, most laptop microphones do not deliver the performance needed for a great video. If it is within your budget constraints, I strongly recommend that you purchase a well-reviewed external microphone. A quality microphone is an excellent investment, one that will pay for itself many times over throughout your freelance career. You will use it for video calls, etc.

Background

You will need a suitable background, one that does not distract the viewer from your message, so avoid a cluttered background. If you can't get a background you're happy with, consider a software program that will remove your background and replace it with whatever you want. Xsplit Vcam is one that I have used in the past, and it works very well. Xsplit Vcam will remove your background and replace it with any image you want as your background.

CONVEYING THE RIGHT MESSAGE

I've broken this down into four steps.

Grab the viewer's attention in the first few seconds of your video.

We know this as *the hook*! Include something in the first few seconds of your video that commands the viewer's attention, piques their interest, or their curiosity. This is going to vary based on your niche. For example, a proofreader may begin by saying, "Do you know why it is so difficult to find errors in your own writing?" Opening with a question is a common tactic for hooks.

Create an emotional connection.

Remember what I said in the chapter titled, *How to Command a Premium Price While Getting More and Better Clients*—people don't buy a service; they buy a story. A story creates an emotional connection with the viewer. Give the viewer an experience, a story in which they can see themselves and that tells them who you are. I'm not suggesting that you weave a story that tugs at their heartstrings. Instead, I want you to simply and effectively convey what drives you to do what you do, and how you came to be in your field of expertise. People want a mirror, so give it to them.

Motivate the viewer to take action.

You want prospects to not only watch your video but also be compelled to take action. The emotional connection does a lot of this work, but you need to take it a step further. You've told them why they should hire you, now ask them to hire you.

Over-deliver.

Your video is a visual introduction, and you want yours to be powerful. You are making a first impression with your video, and, as the adage goes, you don't have a second chance to make a first impression. Take the time you need to do it well. In short, over-deliver!

Tips

- Dress professionally, not necessarily a suit and tie, but, for the guys, at the very least a collared shirt, and for the gals, a neat button-down shirt or blouse with or without a blazer.

- Make certain you are well-groomed.

- During the first few seconds of your video, definitely be smiling. It is important to convey a friendly and open demeanor throughout your video, so well-timed, occasional smiles as your video unfolds are also a good idea.

- I suggest avoiding a script. You want your video to be as natural as possible. Instead, using bullet points to remind you of the key points you wish to make, will keep you on target.

- Keep your video short—two to three minutes at most. Otherwise you risk losing the prospect's interest.

- A video thumbnail is the still image that people browsing your profile see before they view it. When you upload your video to YouTube, you can choose a thumbnail from the three options that YouTube generates automatically. Be sure the option you select is the most flattering one available.

- Alternatively, you can create a thumbnail using Canva.com. Canva offers some high-quality free (and paid) templates that you can use to create a custom thumbnail for your profile video, or you can contract an Upwork freelancer to do it for you.

- Don't create an overly produced video with special effects and don't use an animated explainer video that doesn't show your face.

- If you cannot afford Xsplit Vcam to replace your video's background, free options exist. YouTube offers tutorials on the subject. Just search for *how to remove a video background*.

If you follow this advice, you will have a killer video that gets you noticed and lands you more jobs. As with other aspects of your profile, don't be afraid to experiment. Change the thumbnail, or make another video. Keep track of your results and don't make more than one change at a time! Making more than one change at a time will skew your data. For example, if you notice an uptick in job invites one week after changing your headline **and** your video, how can you know which change caused the uptick in invites?

SECTION 4

KEEP

HOW TO GET GREAT REVIEWS AND CRUSH YOUR COMPETITION

Great reviews begin with exceptional work. There are no shortcuts—sorry. You will not get a five-star review unless you've given a five-star performance. Sadly, freelancers must also face the fact that a five-star performance does not guarantee a five-star review—or any review at all!

Before we go any further, let's look at the six performance categories that make up a client's *Public Feedback*. After all, if you don't know what you're going to be graded on, it's hard to prepare for the test! As you see below the client rates freelancers on 1) skills, 2) quality, 3) availability, 4) deadlines, 5) communications, and 6) cooperation. It is important for you to recognize that work quality represents only one-sixth of the overall score.

Job Feedback

Client's feedback

★★★★★ 5.00

Overall rating			5.00
Skills	5.0	Quality	5.0
Availability	5.0	Deadlines	5.0
Communication	5.0	Cooperation	5.0

Arguably, all six of these categories are subjective, except for deadlines. You must *train* your client throughout the course of the contract by reminding them of how important their review is to you. Tell them from day one that you are working for that great review. Every conversation with your client represents an opportunity. For example, when submitting a milestone, ask the client if they are satisfied with the quality of your work, and use the occasion to remind the client of how much importance you attach to a positive review.

Show your skills at every opportunity and, within reason, make sure you are available to address the client's questions, and concerns. Respond quickly to the client and cooperate with your client to the fullest extent possible. Deadlines are critical, so inform your client of the reasons behind any delay you may encounter in meeting that deadline.

Clients that do not leave feedback are problematic. The absence of feedback does not hurt your JSS, but it doesn't advance it either. Upwork has acknowledged the importance of client feedback and automatically *reminds* clients seven days after they end a contract to submit a review. Upwork sends these reminders via email and also via notifications on the client's screen when they log in. Although helpful, it is no substitute for being proactive in your approach to clients.

Remember what you learned in the chapter titled *Avoid Catastrophe: Researching Your Prospect Is the First Crucial Step.* Information in this chapter can help you identify prospects that are unlikely to provide *Public Feedback.*

I want you to tear out this page and hang it on your wall! This 6-point checklist sets the stage for each client to give you that great review.

1.] **Always be honest and straightforward.** Never exaggerate your skills. Set realistic expectations, be clear on pricing, deadlines, and, if applicable, revisions.

2.] **Keep your client informed.** In any relationship, communication is crucial. Keep clients updated on the status of their projects, quickly alert them to any issues that arise, and respond to their questions as quickly as you can. Use these opportunities to seek feedback, ensure you are on the same page as your client, and remind the client of your goal to provide five-star service. Use these hiccups as opportunities to *train* your client.

3.] **Under-promise and over-deliver.** It is always, *always* better to exceed your client's expectations than to disappoint your client with work that does not conform to what you have promised your client. Always look for opportunities to over-perform. In short, try to delight your client rather than simply satisfy your client.

4.] **Take a comprehensive approach.** Show the client that you are committed to the success of the project. Offer meaningful suggestions that advance the client's goals.

5.] **Guarantee your work.** By this, I mean making it clear to your prospect or client that you are committed to delivering five-star work. And, if that requires you to make revisions or re-work some aspects of the job, you will do so. I like to say, "I'm not happy until you're happy."

6.] **Never argue with a client.** There are no winners in this scenario. Rather than arguing, try to see things from their perspective. While it is acceptable to explain your thinking and rationale, don't press your views to the point the client perceives you as argumentative. Instead, ask for direction so you can match their expectations.

When a client ends a contract, always take the time to email or message the client, thank them for the job, express your interest in working for them again, and remind them of how important leaving a review is to your success as a freelancer.

Let me share a tip with you that is best suited to high-value contracts. It has been my *secret* for a very long time.

When creating your proposal, offer a discount for giving a review, don't ask for a five-star review, that would violate Upwork's TOS. In the proposal, give the prospect two options, the first is your full rate, and the second, a discounted rate for leaving a review within one week of completion.

This approach provides two important benefits. First, the prospect almost always selects the discounted option, which all but guarantees they will leave a review. Second, by offering option A and option B, you have deterred the prospect from further negotiation. For example, you don't ask your child what they want for breakfast. You ask your child if they want oatmeal or pancakes. Asking them an open-ended question will take you into the lunch hour!

When the contract ends, send the client an email similar to the one below.

Thanks again for hiring me. I enjoyed working with you and would love to work with you in the future. As you know, we made an agreement while creating the scope of this project to leave an Upwork review within one week. Please leave your Upwork review as soon as possible. If you felt I did a great job for you, I look forward to reading your positive review.

I've enjoyed phenomenal success with this approach, and I'm happy to share this tip with you.

A closing thought. If you feel you did less than great on a contract (it happens), then give the client the benefit of the discount and tell him not to bother with a review.

PRIVATE VS. PUBLIC FEEDBACK: HOW TO SEPARATE FACT FROM FICTION

I'm sure that, by now, you are clear on the fact that you can improve your JSS based upon positive *public* and *private* feedback from one or more clients, and your JSS may also decline because of poor *public* or *private* feedback. You also understand that feedback, *public* and *private*, carries more weight with the Upwork algorithm when it pertains to a high-value job as opposed to a low-value job.

Since *public* and *private* feedback are two factors impacting your overall JSS, it is a topic worth looking at again. Even though we have previously touched on this subject, the subject is sufficiently important to be worthy of a second look.

In 2015, John J. Horton (Leonard N. Stern School of Business—New York University) and Joseph M. Golden (University of Michigan and Elance/oDesk) published a research document titled *Reputation Inflation in an Online Marketplace*. You can download the paper from the Internet as a PDF. It is a technically difficult but fascinating read.

But first, a brief history. A few years ago, two of the largest freelance platforms were oDesk and Elance. Late in the first half of 2014, these companies announced they would merge into a single company under the oDesk banner. About one year later, they announced a relaunch under the name Upwork, with a new platform of the same name. Upwork promised to combine the best of oDesk and Elance plus innovations. One of those innovations was an enhanced algorithm to improve the site's ability to match freelancers and clients. *Private* and *public* feedback play significant roles in this algorithm, which is why I am including this chapter.

I offer you a summary of the researchers' conclusions below, but you can download it for free and read it yourself.

Summary

The researchers saw that average public feedback scores given to freelancers had strongly increased over time, and no marketplace changes or improvements in performance could adequately explain the change. Researchers offered two theories to explain this, "(1) it costs more to give bad feedback than good feedback when feedback is *public* because buyers fear retaliation and (2) this cost is increasing in the market's average [*public*] feedback score. Together, (1) & (2) push the market towards an equilibrium where feedback is always positive, regardless of performance. To address this problem, the marketplace allowed and encouraged buyers to additionally give *private* feedback. This private feedback was more candid and more predictive of future worker performance. The marketplace experimentally revealed aggregate *private* feedback scores which influenced employers' hiring decisions."

Reputation Inflation in an Online Marketplace explains the reasons Upwork includes private feedback for clients and freelancers alike. It also explains why feedback, both *public* and *private*, play significant roles in your JSS.

HOW TO COMMAND A PREMIUM PRICE WHILE GETTING MORE AND BETTER CLIENTS

I thought about calling this chapter *Sell Me This Pen*, a reference to the iconic movie, *The Wolf of Wall Street*, which is based upon the life of Jordan Belfort. However, Belfort was an unsavory character, a criminal actually, so I decided against it. However, there are lessons to be learned from even the worst of people.

Sell Me This Pen Teaches Freelancers Important Lessons

People buy because of emotion and then try to justify it with logic.

Here's a real-life example. A potential customer had emailed me with dozens of questions regarding my *Upwork Mastery Class*. One week later, his order had not materialized. So, I emailed him to see what happened. "Oh!" he responded, "I'm broke. I just spent $700 on a new iPhone." He tried to justify his purchase with logic, suggesting that his new iPhone would allow him to respond quickly to clients and communicate more effectively.

Of course, his logic is highly flawed. Rather than spending a few bucks for a course that would enable him to earn thousands, he spends his last $700 on a new phone and has no clients! Go figure.

People don't buy into a product or service; they are buying their way out of something.

Successful travel agents, for example, don't sell destinations based on clear blue seas, sunny skies, and pristine white sand beaches. They sell escapes—escape from stress, escape from the daily grind, etc.

People don't buy a service; they buy a story.

Your years of experience, your stellar academic credentials, and your monotonous list of skills will not be long remembered by a prospect. However, if you convert your value into a compelling story that explains why you do what you do, they will never forget you.

It's All about Perception

You must create a perception of value; the value of the work you create. If you want to earn higher fees, then focus on providing and communicating your value to prospects and clients. Communicating is the key word!

Experiment!

I've told you, throughout this book, about the value I place on testing and experimentation. Here's what happened when I experimented with my hourly rate.

I started my freelance career charging $85/hour. Then, overnight, I changed it up to $150/hour, and today my rate is $350/hour. This experimentation produced the following results:

- I landed more clients.
- These clients were superior in quality.
- My clients were less inclined to micro-manage my work.
- I logged more billable hours.

It turns out that my higher hourly rate instilled confidence in the prospect, and increased their level of trust in my abilities. Your fees are rarely the determining factor for landing a job. Instead, the determining factor is that you create value, *and* a perception of value, that aligns with your hourly rate. Focus on providing and communicating more value. That is key!

How Do I Command a Premium Price?

Begin by listing a minimum of twenty benefits that your clients receive because they chose you as their freelancer. By doing this exercise, you learn that the value you provide your clients is worth substantially more than what you are charging (even if you raise your rate), and it changes your entire outlook on freelancing. Importantly, it also informs you on what you need to measure so that you can better communicate your value to prospects. For example, if you are a writer specializing in website copywriting, you can measure the increase in conversions on your client's website.

Make sure that you have defined your niche. Refresh your memory by reviewing *Pick a Niche*, in the *Attract* section of this book. A niche turns you into a specialist and attracts prospects that are looking for solutions to specific problems. The more closely your niche aligns with a prospect's needs, the greater your perceived value becomes to that prospect. So, don't be a blog writer, be a blog writer specializing in pet related content, not a marketing expert, but a marketing expert for SaaS enterprises, or, rather than being a graphic designer, be a graphic designer specializing in product packaging.

Finally, sell benefits, not features. This is key. Your focus should be less on what you do, and much more on how the benefit of what you do impacts the prospect. For example, a virtual assistant explains they can check your emails and respond to customer enquiries.

What the virtual assistant should say is that I can save you hours of your time every week. After all, prospects usually have only two objectives: 1) make a butt load of cash, and 2) save time so that they can make even more cash.

Earlier, I asked you to list a minimum of twenty benefits your clients receive from your work, now I am asking you to memorize that list. Why? If you memorize the benefits, the less likely it is that you will focus on features in your communications with prospects.

HOW TO AVOID PROBLEMS WITH CLIENTS

Avoiding problems with clients begins with avoiding problem clients, as outlined in the chapter, *Avoid Catastrophe: Researching Your Prospect Is the First Crucial Step*. That said, freelancers can take additional steps to avoid problems with clients. Here are six proactive steps you can take.

1.] Be wary of job postings that lack a detailed description of the work expected of you. Equally troubling are ambiguous job postings—postings, for example, that cause you to wonder if the prospect is looking for an editor or a ghostwriter.

2.] These types of job postings should raise a red flag. You will probably end up wasting a lot of time and money when you accept such jobs. Always insist that such prospects clarify their expectations before you agree to a contract.

3.] I deplore job postings that contain the phrase, *easy work*. If it's easy, why doesn't the prospect just do it? More to the point, these individuals place little or no value on what you do.

4.] The same goes for prospects who suggest that the proposed job should only take *a short time*, *is a few minutes' work*, or can be completed *in less than an hour*. If that were true, why would a prospect spend any time at all placing a job post, when they could simply use that time to do the job?

5.] Clients that try to micromanage your work can stress and frustrate you. Too often, this discourages you from delivering your best work, because the client has taken away your ability to explore other, possibly superior, solutions. Set limits for your client from day one. If you get in the habit of responding to emails or messages at midnight, you are toast.

6.] Clients that can't or won't communicate with you are obstacles to your success. Too often this problem isn't discovered until the work has begun. Look for hints in the clients' past reviews from other freelancers.

7.] Avoid prospects who clearly express a preference for the cheapest option. As a freelancer, you should be proud of the service you provide and the benefits you extend to your clients. Prospects who seek the cheapest option do not value your, nor do they value their business.

8.] Clients that are slow to release funds after a job is completed can be very annoying, especially if you have been rushed to complete the job. There isn't much you can do about clients like this except to refuse their work going forward.

WHAT TO DO WHEN THE FIT HITS THE SHAN

Eventually, you're going to encounter a client that makes your life a living hell. It isn't a question of if it's going to happen, but when—and this chapter of the book will help you navigate the experience.

I firmly believe that prevention is the best cure, which is why *Avoid Catastrophe: Researching Your Prospect Is the First Crucial Step* is such an important chapter. However, nothing is foolproof and, no matter how carefully you vet a prospect, a difficult client will eventually slip past you and the fit is going to hit the shan.

Difficult clients broadcast warning signs:

- The client becomes unresponsive. This can slow your progress on a job and slowed progress can give rise to additional problems you wouldn't otherwise need to address, such as deadlines.

- They are clingy. If a client is reaching out to you constantly for no valid reason, don't make the mistake of responding too quickly. This will encourage only more unwanted contact.

- The client has high expectations for your availability. This has ties to the *clingy* client. Just because you have a contract with a client, you have no obligation to be available to that client 24/7.

It is always a good idea to let clients know your windows of availability.

- Scope Creep! This is when a client asks you to perform work above and beyond what they have agreed upon in the contract. And yes, it happens frequently.

- They ask you for free work. This is a huge warning sign! It suggests they do not value your work, or they hate to spend money.

- The client frequently questions your rate or your billable hours. Not only is this irritating, it wastes valuable time. Questions regarding your rate—refer the client to the contract. Questionings regarding the validity of hours billed are an insult to your integrity. It is very difficult to be productive in an atmosphere of mistrust. This may be a point at which you consider ending the relationship. Always consult your contract and review the termination clause before you act.

- Clients, especially those who do not understand what you do, often have unrealistic expectations regarding turnaround times (TAT). You need to communicate your concerns to the client immediately.

- Worse than not understanding what you do, is the client who does not know what he/she wants. This may mean they aren't reviewing your work, or they only know what they need as an end result.

- Clients who complain about other freelancers will complain about you too. This negative energy will only diminish your positive energy.

- Vague answers or an unwillingness to answer your questions are problematic. This often means that the client doesn't want to risk giving a wrong answer, preferring to allow you to take the blame if something goes awry.

- Exercise caution with a client that questions almost every line of a contract. Sure, one or two items may warrant discussion, but beyond that is being unreasonable. Other clients may want you to sign *their* contract. This is not a good idea.

- Sometimes a client just gives off a bad vibe. In my experience, it is always a good idea to follow your gut instincts.

- Nitpicking clients will suck the life right out of you.

- Clients that micromanage will cost you your sanity.

- Paying late, or worse yet, not paying at all, is all the justification you need to part ways with a client.

- Clients that refuse to pay a portion of your fee upfront represent 80 percent of the clients on my *Bad Client List*. Need I say more?

Interventions that May Resolve Problems

- Reaffirm expectations. Do so early and with whatever frequency the circumstances demand. In severe cases, create additional, lower value milestones. By doing this, if you must end the contract, at least you've cut your losses.

- Non-payment is an extreme case. So, when it gets hairy, demand payment, or consider stopping work altogether.

- In certain instances, you need to decide to cut your losses. While ending a contract prior to its completion may seem unprofessional, it may be the best course of action because the client is such a headache.

- Maybe it's my military background, but I always write up an After Action Review (AAR) when I end a job with a client that went badly. It is important to document the events that led to this.

How to Get Rid of Hard to Deal with Clients

1.] In a worst-case scenario, you may unilaterally end the contract. This will trigger the client to request a refund if the contract is fixed price. I encourage you to follow up with a message to the client explaining your reason for ending the contract. This will also become a record for future reference.

2.] Maintain your integrity. If you receive a harsh email response to the termination, avoid that knee-jerk reaction to respond in kind. Always remember that tone can sometimes be difficult to assess in written communications, so,

3.] Always be polite and professional. For example, when you receive an email that upsets or angers you, wait a few hours before responding. Let your temper cool, formulate your response, and then reply. It is amazing the clarity you can achieve when you are not trying to peer through an angry red haze.

4.] Written records are invaluable. Maintain everything in writing, even phone conversations via a transcript.

5.] Keep any further engagement with the former client to a minimum and always stick to facts. Do not make the mistake of becoming emotional. Just the facts!

Personality Types

I thought I'd share some personality traits often associated with problem clients. I stumbled onto these at https://www.practiceignition.com.

- **Party-member Patrick:** He can't make a single decision without consulting with someone back in his office.

- **Know-it-all Nancy:** She knows your business better than you do and she'll tell you everything you're doing wrong at the top of her lungs until you wonder why she's bothering to hire you in the first place.

- **It's a simple job Jason:** Declaring that everything is simple and easy and you won't have any trouble, while asking for a million customized details and complex systems.

- **Emergency Edith:** Everything needs to be done yesterday. Edith has no concept of the fact you have other clients and expects you to bend the space-time continuum to meet her impossible deadlines.

- **Bitching about the bill, Bill:** Bill scrutinizes every detail of your invoice and tries to eke out as much free work as possible.

- **Terrible Terry:** Terry screams down the phone at your staff members and berates you in public over seemingly minor issues about your work. You sleep with one eye open.

Over the course of my freelance career, I've dealt with all of these personality types. Perhaps you have too. If not, I can almost guarantee that you will. Just make sure you see the early warning signs.

HOW TO KEEP CLIENTS AND PROSPECTS HAPPY WITH THE "I NOTICED" APPROACH

Samuel Goldwyn, the *G* in MGM, once said, "When someone does something well, applaud! You will make two people happy." Samuel Goldwyn was on to something! Jorge Moll and his colleagues at the National Institutes of Health conducted a study in 2006 which found that giving [a compliment] activates regions of the brain associated with social connection, trust and pleasure. The recipient of a sincere compliment (client or prospect) also feels happy—happy to be **noticed**! As a freelancer, you know all too well that compliments are hard to come by. Think about it for a moment. As children, we frequently received praise from our parents, but as adults, praise is a comparatively scarce commodity. This is the reason the *I Noticed* approach is so effective.

Imagine the effect a little flattery can have on a prospect (most are adults) that probably haven't heard a kind word in days. Believe me—it's powerful! I've touched on this before in the chapter, *How to Create High Converting Proposals that Will Wow Your Prospects*, but it's important, so I'm going to expand on the subject.

Complimenting a prospect can be helpful or unhelpful, depending on your approach. If you can find nothing to praise in the prospect's proposal, you certainly shouldn't invent an insincere or over-the-top compliment! That will only call your credibility into question. Instead, take the time to do a little research on the prospect and find something that you can flatter—their website, their LinkedIn profile, their freelancer reviews, or something else positive you may learn about the prospect in a Google search.

It is equally important to compliment your client. Compliments are not only a factor in landing a job, they are a factor in retaining clients and developing long-term relationships, which are extremely important in terms of your earning potential, not to mention your JSS.

Here are five tips to keep you on point in the flattery department:

1.] Only compliment professional effort. Avoid praising inconsequential or irrelevant information you may learn about a prospect or client. For example, it's fine to compliment a recent award they received, but it is inappropriate to compliment the tie they wore in their photo.

2.] Ask for advice, but not on the subject matter for which you were hired, because that would show incompetence. While not strictly a compliment, asking for advice shows that you respect them and value their opinion, which suggests that you have professional ambitions. For example, you might say, "I'm impressed with the charts and graphs you've used in your project. May I ask where you learned this skill?"

3.] Always keep your compliments sincere and professional. Avoid overused phrases like "Good job!" or "Nice work!" These can come across as insincere simply because they are overused, nor do they feel tailored to the situation. Use words such as exceptional, terrific, tremendous, or fantastic instead of great. Replace nice with kind, delightful, lovely, or charming, for example.

4.] You should never offer compliments at another's expense. Putting someone else down to lift-up your prospect or your client is always a bad idea. This can foster mistrust, which is the exact opposite of what you want to accomplish. For example, you shouldn't say, "My last client was clueless regarding what needed to be done, but you have outlined the project beautifully!" What if your last client turned out to be this client's business partner!

5.] Don't go overboard! There is a fine line between giving a sincere, well-deserved, well-timed compliment and sounding ridiculous. Use professional verbiage, be brief, and to the point. For example, rather than saying, "Wow, that's a cool idea! Sure is going to save us lots of time." you should say, "That is an impressive idea, and it will definitely enhance our efficiency."

Your key takeaway in this chapter is that landing the interview, and being awarded the contract are only stepping stones to your eventual goal, which is only achieved through your ability to develop a mutually rewarding, long-term relationship with your client.

Look, it's like this. You ask a girl out, she says yes. Then you find that you really like her. Later, you fall in love and your goal is to marry. After you're married do you stop complimenting her? Do you quit surprising her with small gifts? Will you never again bring her flowers? Of course not! I'm no marriage counselor, but I'm reasonably certain that continuing to do what makes her happy is the best course of action.

This isn't so different from a client relationship, which is also hard won, and once won, you must continue to nurture it or you *will* lose it.

THE ART OF DEVELOPING STRONG, PROFITABLE, AND LASTING CLIENT RELATIONSHIPS

Landing a client is an expensive proposition. Even though Upwork shoulders marketing expenses, freelancers spend much of their own time and energy in prospecting for jobs, enhancing their profiles, and brainstorming improvements in their proposals. I've emphasized the importance of prospecting frequently throughout the book, even encouraging you to work only 4 to 6 hours per day so that you will have time to prospect. Let's be frank, time is money!

Did you know that it is nineteen times harder to land a new client than it is to keep an existing client? Let *that* sink in for a minute!

Not surprisingly, there are several reasons you need to care about existing customers:

- Better conversion rates. Existing clients are already sold on you and your services.

- Less marketing effort and expense because they already know your value.

- Higher profitability because they will pay what you are worth.

- No learning curve. You're already familiar with the client and/or business.

- Enhanced opportunities to cross sell and/or up sell your services.

This is a good time to examine the reasons you might lose a customer. According to SuperOffice.com, 1 percent are lost because of death, 3 percent leave the market, 5 percent choose a friend to provide the service, 9 percent are won over by a competitor, 14 percent are dissatisfied with your service, and 68 percent believe you don't care about them.

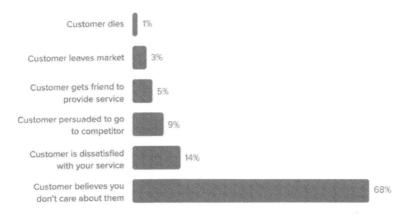

Source: https://www.superoffice.com/blog/customer-retention-tips-with-crm-software

Having read this book, you should not be losing 14 percent of your clients because they are dissatisfied with your service! If you are losing clients for this reason, you have a fundamental problem with the quality of your service and/or communications. If you have followed my advice and maintained after action reviews (AAR) as suggested in *What to Do When the Fit Hits the Shan*, you won't have this problem.

This begs the question, "How do I, as a freelancer, show my clients that I care?"

1.] Avoid becoming dependent on the client's help to get the job done. Sure, clients want to help, but that help is limited to providing you with information, needed passwords, and access. I call this managing up, which means getting everything you need to do the job up front from your client. They do not want to help you do the work. That's why they hired you in the first place!

2.] Inspect what you expect! Measure everything you can. There is no more convincing way to show clients that you have made a positive impact than by giving them cold, hard facts. Being able to show your value to a client is key to keeping that client. For example, if you're a writer writing a blog post for an ecommerce client. Take baseline stats to note the conversions of previous blog posts on their website to the product page. Then note *your* stats. If your conversion rates are higher, that means higher revenue for the client which enhances your value and increases your chance of not only getting more work, but being able to charge more.

3.] Make your schedule transparent to your clients. Nothing POs a client more than your unscheduled absence.

4.] Always under promise and over deliver. Words to live by!

5.] Meet/communicate regularly with your client.

6.] Ask your client how (stats, video, images, etc.) and how often they would like to be updated. What's reasonable will vary from job to job. The important take-away is that you need to set expectations regarding frequency and establish in advance the day and time this should take place.

7.] Make your clients aware of *all* your skill sets. If your clients are aware of your capabilities, you may not need to up sell or cross sell them, they will up buy and cross buy with you. More importantly, your clients won't be looking for other freelancers to do what they know you are perfectly capable of doing.

8.] Maybe a gift? It's a great way to kick-off a large project, and I almost always gift a client for referrals. It need not be an expensive gift—something as simple as a $10 Starbucks gift card.

9.] Be overly nice, not only polite, but really, really nice—even if it is a one-way street. This includes owning your mistakes. Don't blame the client, your subordinate, or make lame excuses. Owning your mistakes (and we all make them) will earn your clients' respect.

Following all or most of these suggestions will all but guarantee you a fantastic client retention rate.

HOW TO HAVE GREAT CLIENT COMMUNICATIONS WITHOUT SACRIFICING YOUR SANITY

I'm going to begin this chapter by addressing a pet peeve I have with Upwork's messaging system. A simple settings change will dramatically reduce the number of messages you send and, if you share this tip with your clients, it will cut the number of messages/email notifications you receive—by half or more!

Do you see the gear icon in the message box? Click on it!

This will open the dialogue box you see below.

The first arrow points to the default setting. With this setting, each time you press enter/return, you send a message. If you're composing a message containing four or five sentences, your client will receive four or five email notifications. How annoying is that?

With a click on the radio button to the left of the second arrow, you eliminate this annoying feature, while, at the same time, eliminating the flurry of email notifications your client receives.

You can always use **Shift+Enter** or **Ctrl+Enter** to type multi-line messages.

Choosing this setting means you must use the send icon (right arrow) to forward your message (see below). Clicking on the phone icon (left arrow), allows you to begin a Zoom, Upwork, or phone call.

You can also access this and other settings by clicking the gear icon that appears above your message list.

Don't forget—share this tip with your clients! You deserve your sanity as well.

Another feature, that can save you some embarrassment, is activated by a click on the gear icon in a previously sent message. When clicked, a drop-down box gives you the option to delete the message. This can be a lifesaver!

Upwork provides all the communication tools you need. Never use Skype or WhatsApp. First, it violates Upwork's TOS to engage in off-platform communications with prospects before the hire. Second, external communication tools such as these are productivity killers. Two of the very worst are Slack and text messaging.

Slack is a major productivity killer, and it destroys your ability to maintain focus. Clients expect an immediate response, which makes the use of Slack a major distraction. Slack is not designed for task management, although many companies try to use it for that purpose. Slack is more like a giant chatroom, offering little direction and lots of distraction. You will be bombarded with notifications and possibly earn your client's ill will by not following up as fast as your client expects. Slack will crush your soul with an avalanche of notifications. If a client wants you to use Slack, politely but firmly decline. Inform your client that the only communication you use outside the Upwork platform is email.

Text messaging has similar drawbacks. Clients expect immediate responses and lose all respect for your hours and your time. Like Slack, you can't flag action items for follow-up and you certainly can't remember the details of all the texts you receive. Again, politely inform your client that email is the only acceptable off-platform means of communication.

SECTION 5

CLOSE

4 UPWORK MEGA EARNERS SHARE THEIR STORIES AND REVEAL THEIR SUCCESS TIPS

I asked four Upwork mega earners to share their top Upwork tips. It is common knowledge that if you want to be successful, you need to learn from and be around successful people. Well, here is your chance to learn from the top earners on Upwork.

Name: Courtney Allen
Upwork Profile: https://www.upwork.com/fl/courtneyallen
Lifetime Earnings: $1M+
Hourly Rate: $125.00
Specialty: Presentations - PowerPoint Wizard
Website: www.16X9design.com

Courtney A.

📍 Atlanta, United States – 6:11am local time

97%

Job Success

🛡 EXPERT-VETTED

Lovingly bestowed the title of PowerPoint Wizard from past clients, I've been a presentation specialist full-time for eight years. That's a fancy way of saying I beautify slide decks for a living. In 2016 I hopped into freelance work full time. Through Upwork I've gotten incredible opportunities to work with Microsoft as an Art Director to oversee template creation for Office 365, design event templates for Adobe, remaster dozens of sales training modules for Yelp and Red Bull, connect with clients across three dozen countries, and help startups raise millions in investment funding.

I build templates from the standpoint of their usability, align training modules into new branding, and am the late-night hero who will turn your keynote or pitch deck into polished goods overnight. Having clients feeling prepared and confident is a job well done.

But you don't get to managing 300 clients a year without some stumbles and falls along the way. Having a heavy workload and high expectations is like a game of Tetris—sometimes you miss your mark. Just recently I replicated a client's beautiful website in presentation form. Thinking that's what he wanted. He retorted that his company's tagline is «Don't copy, create» and asked for a refund. Ouch.

However, through years of trial and error, I've picked up a few things. Here are my Top 5 Tips for finding success on Upwork.

1.] **Setting client expectations.** I attribute my success freelancing to client management more than my design capabilities. Before signing a contract, I send over a written proposal with detailed scope (and specifying what's out of scope), timeline, and budget to ensure we're in full agreement. If I expect any adjustments needing to be made to deadlines and especially to the cost, I inform the client in advance for approval. Having the project requirements is important for flat-rate projects, where scope creep is the name of the game. If we're exceeding the initial parameters of the project, I can quickly inform the client of any potential additional fees. Clients really appreciate the transparency throughout the process. As another example of setting expectations, if they're looking for a super quick turnaround, I always enforce a rush fee... that quickly separates those who needed it done "yesterday" versus tomorrow.

2.] **Be reliable.** The reason I keep 65% of my clients for repeat work is that I'm always consistent and on time in my deliverables. Like your favorite meal, it never gets old. I often hear complaints from clients that their original go-to designer takes days, even weeks to respond to emails or turn around tasks, and they finally got frustrated and looked elsewhere. Although I work with up to two dozen clients at one time, I always try to make each one feel prioritized and respond to their messages in a timely manner.

3.] **Provide a WIP draft.** I adopted this practice a few years ago and never looked back. You don't want to waste your client's budget or your time on work that isn't approved. Get a temperature check midway through a first-draft—clients like being active participants. I've found that clients are very receptive to me creating several initial options for them to choose from, even at an additional cost. Win-win.

4.] **Learn to estimate your projects accurately.** I still struggle with this but have learned some methods of becoming more accurate with your bids.

- Don't be afraid to estimate higher than the budgeted amount or hourly rate listed in the job posting, *especially* if you are invited to the job.

- When determining your rate for a flat fee, always add at least 10-15% above your hourly rate X hours you think it'll take, *particularly* if they're a new client.

- If you want to go above and beyond, keep a spreadsheet of clients, total budget, and hours worked to get your effective hourly rate. I've been doing this for the past several months and in horror realized a $5000 project ended up with me making about $10/hr. It really puts things in perspective and helps you realize where and how you might be underestimating.

5.] **Not all money is good money.** Be very selective in what projects or clients you take on. I always pre-screen potential new clients—I read their reviews to see if other freelancers have flagged them for lack of communication or payment in the past, assess their experience on the platform, and see if their average rate paid on past projects is in the ballpark of my hourly rate. Don't accept lowball offers, provide free work, or endure poor attitudes. And if you encounter the latter mid-project, learn to walk away with grace—the stress isn't worth the money, trust me.

Name: Olzhas Alexandrov
Lifetime Earnings: $800k+
Hourly Rate: $150.00
Upwork Profile: https://www.upwork.com/o/profiles/users/~018e2d48fa8a42e825
Specialty: Full Stack Developer
Website: N/A

Olzhas A. ✅

📍 Dallas, United States – 5:05am local time

99%
Job Success

🛡 **TOP RATED PLUS**

Hello, my name is Olzhas, a full-stack developer who specializes on the web, mobile, and desktop applications distributed as websites and through the app stores. My working niche is broad as I need to provide clients with infrastructure and backend solutions that power the client-facing applications for various platforms. To cover such scope, I continuously attempt to generalize and standardize the workflows that I offer. That is how I ended up as a full-stack developer who primarily specializes on the event-driven web-based solutions that are distributable to any platform (device). Whereas on the infrastructure, I have experimented with various providers and different approaches and ended up specializing in Amazon Web Services (AWS) defining infrastructure as code and creating serverless event-driven solutions. To date, I completed over 115 contracts with over 10 thousand hours and overall earnings of about one million dollars on Upwork. I got certified by AWS by taking all the highest possible professional AWS exams (Solutions Architect and DevOps Engineer) scoring almost the highest possible scores on those exams and also got certified in AWS Machine Learning Specialty.

Overall, my experience on Upwork is a cheerful story and I honestly do not feel any pressure or stumble upon any difficulties nowadays. However, my first probably 60 contracts were not always pleasant and to be more transparent, I almost constantly was under stress. The stress was about different aspects of a freelancer's lifestyle: the necessity to find contracts, the desire to work on contracts that bring an opportunity to further polish skills, the unpredictability of contracts, the necessity to always be psychologically stable and prepared for all possibilities, etc. Looking back, I believe I never really had any unsolvable situations, or zugzwang, and everything in the past now seems pretty normal and simple to solve.

Let me please attempt to share my top five tips for finding success on Upwork. I direct the tips to my former self; I know these tips would have helped me back then:

1. Self-presentation

Self-presentation includes everything about your profile, you, and the way you communicate with the client. The bad part is it takes time to identify the aspects that apply to your particular niche, you, and your clients. The good part is you are completely in control of how well you present yourself. As with everything else, if you are just beginning your journey, start by identifying the best professionals in your niche and copy everything they do. If you are not a beginner, still monitor top professionals' workflows to be informed about potential optimization opportunities. As time goes on, stay open-minded and question every aspect of your previous decisions in this area. Such a detail-oriented approach would positively make you stand out among the professionals in your niche.

2. Set client's success as your number one priority

If you genuinely attempt to solve clients' cases by trying to bring value with every message and action on the client's project, the probability to fail in a project would drastically decrease. Many employees do not make the client their number one priority, then the client feels it and those employees become one step out of the project.

3. Continuously network and search for new opportunities

Even if you do your work perfectly, there is still the risk of losing a job because of various possibilities that are out of your control. Rarely, but especially during economic recessions, the clients' or their representatives might not inform you of their hardships, trying to not distract you from work. It is important to always be on guard and prepared for such cases by either constantly having options for new opportunities, or splitting your working time between clients, so you diversify such risks.

4. Communication

Almost every freelancer understands the importance of keeping the client up to date in terms of the progress, potential obstacles, and other notable aspects of the workflow. However, the typical case when knowing what is right and doing that rarely align is in times of hardships. Freelancers, as any other people, have a natural desire to communicate only positive news, which results in poor communication. There are two strategies that help me the most in such cases:

- Plan the communication as detailed as possible. It would help you rid yourself of all emotional/feelings related weaknesses as you would worry less with a more predictable workflow because of having a planned course of action for different communication scenarios.

- Attempt to do your best while looking at everything from a third-person point of view. It does not mean that you should not care about the client, this mentality keeps your head cool at all times.

5. Analyze your rate

Whenever you start, you set your first appraisal of yourself as a resource by setting your rate. Then, as you work for clients, you will receive other offers. The longer you are in your industry, the more you understand the demand. The simplest way to set an appropriate price tag on your services is by decreasing the rate when no one is hiring and increasing the rate when you receive too many offers and proposals. Sometimes, you might feel discouraged when clients are unwilling to hire. Treat this as a sign to improve not only professional skills but also every other aspect of your self-presentation. Continuously work on improving every nuance of your services and self-presentation.

Name: Jaime Hollander
Lifetime Earnings: $1M+
Hourly Rate: $250.00
Upwork Profile: http://www.upwork.com/fl/jaimeh2
Specialty: Content Strategist and Copywriter
Website: https://rrdali.com

Jaime H. ✅

📍 Glen Head, United States - 6:20am local time

99%
Job Success

🛡 EXPERT-VETTED

I'm Jaime Hollander and I'm a Content Strategist and Copywriter on Upwork. I first joined the platform—then Elance—in September 2012. My background is in media and magazine publishing, having worked at Conde Nast Publications, Meredith Corporation, Time Out New York, and more. Since joining Upwork, I've worked with Fortune 500 companies and enterprise leaders in countless industries.

In terms of terrible experiences that became learning experiences, I have a few. Most, though, come back to accepting the WRONG jobs with the WRONG clients—typically jobs I felt unsure about going in.

While this has happened a few times—and I've learned! One case in particular stands out. A client was vulgar via email and on our pre-hire/interview calls. He hated my work, criticized everything, said I was too expensive, and objected to my initial suggestions. We also had a significant language barrier, and he'd often correct my work—but his corrections weren't "correct," and he'd get angry when I pushed back.

In short, he was rude. But the budget was VERY high, I was a newbie to freelancing, had bandwidth—so, when he hired me, I dove in.

The project was a disaster. He would approve content then, days later, rip it apart and tell me he hated it. He would "correct" my copy, making it worse (or, most times, incorrect), then yell when I pushed back on his changes. He was rude and resorted to name-calling very quickly. I spent close to 100 hours and I wound up walking away, making nothing.

There are several other examples like this — each cost me time (and other jobs...) and caused unnecessary anxiety, stress, and frustration. Now, I trust my gut—even if I really want the job.

Some notes on this...

- In freelancing (especially in the beginning), there's a genuine feeling of scarcity—that you have to take EVERY job that comes your way because there might not be another. I get it. I was in the same boat—and, honestly, I still have to fight the "yes" urge sometimes. But BE SMART. Yes, in the beginning you SHOULD be focused on building your portfolio, you DO NOT (and should not) say yes to everything. Sometimes a client isn't a good fit—or you can tell you aren't a good fit for that client. If you think you can make it work, great. If, though, you're feeling apprehensive or flat-out know it's a poor fit, AVOID. Chances are, this contract will cause you more stress, frustration, and disappointment. Move on and find a new project that sync—and that you can happily deliver on.

- A poor prospect is a bad client. The person who challenges your rate, pushes back and makes you jump through hoops to get a job will not suddenly become a great client. A poor prospect will be a poor client. A good test? If you DREAD seeing an email from a prospect or feel anxious or angry when reading/responding to their messages, move on. It's not worth the angst.

Tips

- Be firm—but flexible—about your rate. Especially in the beginning, be flexible about your rates...to a point. You need to build an Upwork portfolio—it's great you have experience, but your Upwork reviews/ratings matter most in this environment. I recommend setting a low but reasonable rate—in the beginning I charged $25/hour despite having more than a decade of experience in senior-level roles. Each time I booked a new job or two, I raised my rate by $5/hour. When I was fully booked, I increased by rate by $10/hour. That's the process I used—now I bill $250/hour, consistently. That said, I AM flexible if a client needs long-term work or wants to book lots of hours— especially if it's a client I want to work with. All of this said, be firm but flexible. If you're charging $25/hour, don't let a client sell you on making $5/hour. It goes back to scarcity—there's always another job out there. That said, if a client you want to work with has $20/hour budgeted, don't be afraid to say YES. I've had freelancers push back over a few dollars—it's good to know your value, but there's a difference between being flexible and being taken advantage of.

- Be a good partner—but be aware of where the line is. I typically include 2 rounds of revisions in my work—it's important to have a limit. That said, if a client comes back and asks a quick question or wants an alternative title option (or something equally minor), I do it. That's being a good partner. I've had freelancers refuse to make a quick tweak or rephrase a sentence because they've hit their revision limit. I get it—no one likes scope creep but, again, it's about knowing what's being a good partner versus what's being taken advantage of. There's a line—but I always lean back on the Golden Rule. And when it's clearly scope creep? Be sure you outline what's included and what's not upfront in writing—a proposal, email, SOW, etc. That way you can lean on that should the scope start creeping. I wouldn't spring "we're out of revisions!" on your client— remind them, "this is round 1 of revisions—are there any other stakeholders who need to be included?" or "this is the second round of revisions—anything else we'll need before wrapping this draft?"

- Respond to invites professionally. Just because you were invited doesn't mean you have the job. Don't say, "Let's get started." Remind me why I invited you. I probably sent dozens of invites.

- Dedicate the time. In the beginning, I spent 1 hour/day applying for projects. Don't sit back and wait for invites—they aren't coming unless you're an active, successful Upwork freelancer. Commit the time and find/apply for the jobs professionally. THIS is your job until you find a job.

- Don't demand payment until the client approves. We all want to get paid, but requesting payment before the client even looks at your work isn't appropriate and makes it seem more transactional than a true partnership. Be a partner, not a ticket-taker.

- Be open to feedback—and don't be afraid to ask questions if you're unclear. Getting incomplete revisions back is frustrating and slows down the process.

- Expand your reach—but stay in your lane. Upwork clients expect expertise—if you've never used Mailchimp, don't paint yourself as an expert. It's unfair to your paying client and detracts from your reputation and Upwork's.

- Commit the time—in the beginning, I spent 1 hour/day applying to projects. Over time, that became an hour a few times a week, then JUST responding to invites. But too often new freelancers send a few proposals or complain they don't get invites...you REALLY have to put in the time and expect that you won't get responses to most proposals you submit.

- Those proposals need to sell YOU—without making the client work too hard. Hit the highlights in your opening paragraph, then elaborate. Who have you worked for/with? What types of projects do you excel at? What samples did you attach, and how are they relevant to my job post? And don't send 1000 samples... send 3 that really speak to your talent and to the project. Your proposals don't have to be long. They just have to be engaging and show me how I'll benefit from working from you.

- Be willing to work for less—my first job was $20... I wrote a few hundred words to accompany a recipe. I had been in publishing for almost a decade. But the work was quick, and I got a 5-star review within 24 hours. That led to another job with that client, and subsequently, I was able to build my profile. My first rate was $10/hour. I knew I was worth a lot more, but you have to start somewhere. Within a week I was at $15/hour and another week $25/hour. Every time I got a project at a certain rate, I raised my rate $5/hour. Within a year I was at $75/hour. Now I'm at $225/hour. While you might command a lot more in your industry, you're starting over here. THAT SAID, I wouldn't suggest taking on a MASSIVE project for $15/hour, I would recommend doing a quick 1 to 2-hour project for that rate. Get the review. Make the connection. Move on to the next thing. You can do several of those in a week—a day, even—and build your profile FAST.

- Look for red flags, and don't ignore them—scope creep, unrealistic expectations, scam-y clients... unfortunately, they exist everywhere. Do your best to sniff them out. If someone doesn't have time to write a thorough job post, I don't apply. «Write my website» as a job post shows me the person doesn't know what they want. There's a good chance this is someone who will not give good feedback/inputs—these are often difficult clients who, because they don't know what they want, won't be happy with what you produce. Avoid! You're a thoughtful freelancer who deserves thoughtful clients.

- DON'T respond to invites with "thanks for inviting me, I'm interested." I haven't hired you... yet. Submit a thorough proposal, knowing you've already got an edge on the other proposals...

- Be an SME (subject matter expert)—pick an area of focus and start there. Be open, but be respectful that clients are looking for EXPERTS. If you don't know Mailchimp or Instagram or AdWords, don't learn on a client (unless they know you're learning...). There are TONS of jobs on Upwork—focus on the ones you'll enjoy doing and will do well. You'll be happier, less stressed, AND your client will probably be happier with the results.

- Then, once you're hired:

- Lay out a proposed timeline for the client to review/approve.

- Industry-standard is two rounds of revisions (IMO)...be willing to do at least two rounds. I'm usually willing to do a quick «tighten» after that. You want to avoid scope creep, but you ALSO want to be an accommodating partner.

- If you don't understand something, ask questions—and better yet, give an example so I know what you're envisioning.

- Think about what OTHER value you can lend the client. I enjoy having a small circle of freelancers and contractors. If you did a good job and can lend more value to my business, tell me!

- Check in with former clients every few weeks. Some of my favorite clients are long-term clients—we only planned to work together once but, now, 8 years later, we're still chugging along.

Name: Doug Shaw
Lifetime Earnings: $990k+
Hourly Rate: $ 75.00
Upwork profile: https://www.upwork.com/fl/dougs
Specialty: Ads for Google, Facebook, LinkedIn, Apple, YouTube + Tag Manager
Website: N/A

doug s. ⊘

📍 Spring Valley, United States – 3:35am local time

98% 🛡 **EXPERT-VETTED**

Job Success

I have high praise for Upwork, as it truly delivers on its foremost aim - matching job posters with freelance contractors.

If you have big dreams or even modest goals, Upwork provides you the means to achieve either. You can count on Upwork as a mature system that balances both the needs of job posters and contractors. If you read the Wiki and other posts about the firm on the internet, you will find evidence of a deep history, a notable merger and a record of stable, thoughtful, carefully crafted growth. That will give you confidence.

The first step for new users is simply to search current job postings that require your skill set. If there are dozens and dozens of postings going back a couple of weeks, then dig deeper and really size up the demand with more precision and also your eligibility to provide fulfillment. Read the job posts, judge your candidacy, and score your chances.

So, assuming you have a match between what you offer and ample suitors in Upwork, your next step is substantiating your background for your Upwork profile. Most of what you have in your LinkedIn profile will help fill out the basics - and that includes work history, certifications, degrees, testimonials and before-and-after visual representations of successes. After you get all the basics out of the way, hustle and search for job posts that match your skills.

How to Get Jobs

If you prefer regular, and varied work in your field, the foremost tactic you can implement at the beginning is to underprice your service relative to your experience. SMB's who are more mindful of value - will be more inclined to sign up with you. All of us want to catch a rising wave, to get in on the ground floor of a significant investment. That sentiment existing in Upwork favors the job poster.

Many small businesses and start-ups have smaller budgets for contract labor, but still need a job or task done by an expert and lack the internal resources to do so. This group will trade on fewer available bona fides within Upwork, if they can acquire your services at a rate that appears to be conveying a lot of value. I am sure many reading this will be reluctant to lower their rate, but there is a very important side benefit to doing so–the potential of a glowing positive review of your services in Upwork. Reviews of your work in Upwork are currency and the key to your growth.

So, if you are willing to implement this tactic for the next few months, it is time to apply for jobs. Create a boilerplate proposal that summarizes your value proposition and vary it based on the job post. Always address the client's specific needs in your proposal. Ask one or two thoughtful questions that reveal your expertise. Sometimes include a question that elicits a response that allows you to judge them as well. As a digital marketer, I always ask for their website URL. If possible, offer some brief thoughtful advice, owing to your value prop. If you can get a dialogue going, ensure that you respond within a couple hours. Be mindful that you are likely among a half dozen other contractors they are actively considering. Keep a log of the dialogues you make and tally the response rate of your pitches.

The next step is scheduling a call via Upwork to discuss the project in more detail. I strongly suggest that you take a phone call with every potential client. Talking with someone on the phone personalizes the relationship, builds trust going both ways, and allows you to get a better sense of their expertise and their expectations. Their job post is typically far short of an RFP. The phone call provides you a means to get a greater understanding of the client's needs. If you are inclined to proceed with the client, offer to provide a written summary of the tasks performed, what the deliverables or milestones would be, and the timeline to complete. Ask the client to send you an offer.

Getting a great review follows directly from exceeding expectations. So over deliver. That includes providing companion advice beyond the agreed upon deliverable. As a digital marketer, I am charged with setting up advertising campaigns. However, along the way I inevitably discover many things my clients are lacking on their websites or sales funnels. I alert them to these things and that advice is typically greeted warmly.

How to Thrive

Repeat the optimal sequence I described above over several months. Slowly increase your rates. Upwork algorithms will take notice of your results and give you favor. Much like Google.com, Upwork has an algorithm that cedes you in search results on the job poster's side. You will gradually get more invitations to make proposals because of favorable reviews. When this happens, it is a sign that you have made it as a contractor.

Conclusion

There is ample advice within Upwork's official help files and highly active forums. Make a point of understanding of all the ways to position yourself for success. The benefits of providing consistently outstanding work are almost unbounded. There are many achievement levels that lead to more and better opportunities, and higher levels of income as well.

Finally, know the Upwork rules and follow them to the letter. If you end up relying on Upwork as a major source of income, getting suspended or banned because you tried to circumvent their systems will end up as a major regret. The best aspect of Upwork is its many subject areas, and endless pipeline of opportunities. So, keep your eye on the ball and be around for the long term.

MY PROVEN RECIPE FOR LONG-TERM SUCCESS ON THE UPWORK PLATFORM

Your long-term success on Upwork's platform largely depends on understanding and proactively applying the *three pillars* we have discussed at length in the previous pages of this book. They are:

1.] Attract
2.] Convert
3.] Keep

It is no accident that these are the names of three sections in this book. My experience as an *Expert Rated* Upwork freelancer makes it clear to me that long-term success is built on these three pillars.

Attract

You achieve long-term success by selecting the right niche for what you do. Recognizing that what you do, the interests and skills you have, are going to change. We must continually address these changes in every aspect of our profile.

Attracting the right prospects is your mission. Never forget that because it is critical to your long-term success. Your badges, your JSS, your profile, your understanding of the algorithm, and your adherence to Upwork's terms of service all play into your staying power on Upwork's platform.

Convert

Honing your ability to spot potential problem clients, creating exceptional proposals, securing more invitations, setting up RSS feeds (or setting up an account at Vollna.com) that allow you to respond quickly to jobs of interest, conserving current high-value clients using the PML technique, and crafting a profile video that creates interest and emotional connections with prospects are all essential to your long-term success and detailed in the *Convert* section of the book.

Keep

Understanding what is necessary to get awesome reviews; grasping the nuances between *Private* and *Public Feedback*; knowing when to increase your rate and how to leverage that increase to gain more and better clients; learning to spot job posts that signal potential problems with prospects; being well-versed in what to do when a job goes south; and lessons in keeping clients happy are all contained in the *Keep* section of the book.

In short, the recipe for long-term Upwork success is written in the pages of this book. If you follow this recipe—this guide, your long-term success is assured!

SECTION 6

APPENDIX

A CATEGORIZED LIST OF FREELANCING WEBSITES BY NAME AND URL

General Freelance Jobs

Upwork

https://www.upwork.com

FlexJobs
https://www.flexjobs.com

SolidGigs

https://solidgigs.com

Fiverr

https://www.fiverr.com

CloudPeeps

https://www.cloudpeeps.com

Indeed

https://www.indeed.com

College Recruiter

https://www.collegerecruiter.com

Freelancer

https://www.freelancer.com

Guru

https://www.guru.com

ServiceScape

https://www.servicescape.com

Craigslist

https://sfbay.craigslist.org

Freelance Writing Jobs

Contena

https://www.contena.co

Freelance Writing Gigs

https://www.freelancewritinggigs.com

Blogging Pro

https://www.bloggingpro.com/jobs

Journalism Jobs

https://www.journalismjobs.com

Morning Coffee eNewsletter

https://www.freelancewriting.com/newsletters/morning-coffee-jobs-newsletter

Freelance Writing

https://www.freelancewriting.com/jobs

All Indie Writers

https://allfreelancewriting.com/freelance-writing-jobs

Freedom With Writing

http://www.freedomwithwriting.com

MediaBistro

https://www.mediabistro.com/jobs

Paid to Blog

http://paidtoblog.com

Due

https://due.com/guest-post-on-due

Pub Loft

https://publoft.com/writers

Contently

https://contently.com/register

Freelance Design Jobs

99 Designs
https://99designs.com

Behance
https://www.behance.net

Dribbble
https://dribbble.com

AngelList
https://angel.co

Art wanted
https://www.artwanted.com

DesignCrowd
https://www.designcrowd.com

Envatostudio
https://studio.envato.com

Coroflot
https://www.coroflot.com/design-jobs

Smashing Magazine
https://jobs.smashingmagazine.com/jobs

CrowdSPRING
https://www.crowdspring.com

Working Not Working
https://workingnotworking.com

Freelance Developer Jobs

Codeable
https://codeable.io

Gun.io
https://www.gun.io/

Lorem
https://www.storetasker.com

Joomlancers
http://joomlancers.com

Rent a Coder
https://www.rent-acoder.com

10X
https://www.10xmanagement.com

gigster
https://gigster.com

Talent Cupboard
https://www.talentcupboard.com

Programmer Meet Designer
http://www.programmermeetdesigner.com

YouTeam
https://youteam.io

Freelance Photographer Jobs

Craigslist

https://sfbay.craigslist.org

The Creative Loft

https://photography.thecreativeloft.com

Cruise Ship Jobs

https://www.cruiseshipjob.com/photographer-jobs.html

Photography Jobs Central

https://www.creativejobscentral.com/photography-jobs

JournalismJobs

https://www.journalismjobs.com

Thumbtack

https://www.thumbtack.com

Photography Jobs Online

https://www.photography-jobs.net

Freelance Photographer Jobs

https://www.indeed.com

Freelance Marketing Jobs

peopleperhour
https://www.peopleperhour.com

Remotive
https://remotive.io

Aquent
https://aquent.com

Maple
https://www.mayple.com

Virtual Assistant Jobs

Belay
https://belaysolutions.com/our-company

timeetc
https://timeetc.com/us/be-a-virtual-assistant

Clickworker
https://www.clickworker.com

Amazon Mechanical Turk
https://www.mturk.com

VA Networking
https://www.vanetworking.com

Assistant Match

https://assistantmatch.com/become-a-virtual-assistant

Zirtual

https://www.zirtual.com/jobs

Fancy Hands

https://www.fancyhands.com/job/apply

Boldly

https://boldly.com

Freelance Video Editing Jobs

Behance

https://www.behance.net/joblist

Mandy

https://www.mandy.com

ProductionHUB

https://www.productionhub.com/jobs

Stage32

https://www.stage32.com/find-jobs

Assemble

https://www.assemble.tv

Freelance Sales Jobs

ZipRecruiter

https://www.ziprecruiter.com/Jobs/Freelance-Sales-Rep

CommissionCrowd

https://www.commissioncrowd.com/listings/commission-only-sales-opportunities/opportunities

Red Hat

https://www.redhat.com/en

Sales Force App Exchange Job Board

https://appexchange.salesforce.com/jobs

Skipthedrive

https://www.skipthedrive.com/job-category/remote-sales-jobs

Freelance Customer Support Jobs

Workana

https://www.workana.com

We Work Remotely

https://weworkremotely.com

VirtualVocations

https://www.virtualvocations.com/q-telecommuting-customer-service-jobs.html

Support Driven

https://jobs.supportdriven.com